Dependence

ALBERT MEMMI

DEPENDENCE
A Sketch for a Portrait of the Dependent

Translated by Philip A. Facey

Foreword by Fernand Braudel

Beacon Press   Boston

Copyright ©1984 by Beacon Press
Translated by Philip A. Facey from *La Dépendance*
©Editions Gallimard, 1979

Beacon Press books are published under the auspices
of the Unitarian Universalist Association of
Congregations in North America,
25 Beacon Street, Boston, Massachusetts 02108
Published simultaneously in Canada by
Fitzhenry and Whiteside Limited, Toronto
Printed in the United States of America

(paperback) 9   8   7   6   5   4   3   2   1

Library of Congress Cataloging in Publication Data

Memmi, Albert.
    Dependence: a sketch for a portrait of the dependent.

    Translation of: La dépendance.
    1. Dependency (Psychology)   I. Title.
BF575.D34M4513   1984   155.2'32   83-70652
ISBN 0-8070-4301-X (pbk.)

"It is not good that man should be alone... He shall cleave unto his wife, and they shall be one flesh."

—*Genesis 2:18, 24*

"Without me you can do nothing."

—*John 15:5*

"Revolution, I now believe in only you."
—*A Revolutionary song*

"If you don't want to feel the horrible burden of Time breaking your back and bending you down toward the ground, keep yourself drunk.

"But on what? On wine, on poetry, or on virtue, whatever you want. But get drunk."
—*Baudelaire, "Enivrez-vous,"* Le Spleen de Paris, *XXXIII*

"There's no such thing as an adult."

—*André Malraux*

Contents

Dependence

Foreword

This essay by Albert Memmi is remarkable for its striking, "hypnotic" clarity, and genuine simplicity — virtues that everyone who reads it is bound to appreciate.

It is a conquest, a discovery.

But the conquest has always been within our reach; the discovery has always been right there for us to make. All we had to do was open our eyes.

So we are in this book even before we get past the first few lines. Dependence is in us and around us; it envelops and protects us; it is necessary and both a help and a hindrance.

I, personally, am not of course exempt from dependence. I am, we are, you are, everyone is dependent. And the word can just as easily be used in the plural. Not only is there dependence, there are dependencies, which form networks.

There are the people I love and adore, without whom life would be intolerable; there is society with all its enticements; there are my convictions, my ways — my passion for writing, to mention just one. I, like Albert Memmi, will have spent the better part of an already long existence at my writing table, in my library, searching for an indispensable book that I can never find right away or for a word that I need to complete a sentence and that escapes me. That constant dependence has been and is simply monstrous. Sometimes I think society is making a fool of me, sentencing me to hard labor so that, preoccupied with tasks that have become delectable to me, I won't be likely to think about the tragic futility of our fate or to notice the haunting shadow of death. Dependence is thus, like Aesop's tongue, both the best and the worst of things.

Just when we thought we were on a road that would take us straight to our destination, we find ourselves in the middle of a square from which we could go off in a thousand directions. That is why Memmi is trying to help us, to offer us an investi-

Dependence

gation of the problem that approaches it from only three sides. This procedure reduces dependence to just a triangle, whose points are: first, the dependent (I thus begin with myself); then the person on whom I depend, the person I love, the "provider"; and, finally, the dependence itself, the "thing" without which there would be no equilibrium.

I am willing to accept this easy approach, but is it sufficient? Dependence is not limited to individuals. It is a central aspect of contemporary life. It affects society as a whole and, ultimately, the existence of the human race itself.

In that regard, Albert Memmi offers the reader numerous inducements. If you listen to him you will find yourself continually asking questions and frequently rereading his rapid prose. The essence of this book runs through our hands and escapes between our fingers. We can't get a grip on it. Is that deliberate, premeditated, natural? Or is the author inviting us to read the excellent books he has previously written, or, better still, those he plans to write?

Yes, dependence is everywhere, and its influence on our behavior is enduring: colonization, social hierarchy, the struggle between classes and between men and women, and the current state of the world are all reflections of dependence. The reality and the anguish of the world come toward us. And the word *dependence* evokes other words; it immediately confers a special status on the weighty and inevitable concept of *domination*.

Finally, have I been bewitched or am I being carried away simply because I accepted such a direct method of investigation? Dependence gives the social sciences a new sound, new meaning, making us feel as if we had new ears, new eyes, new intellects.

And now I, for all intents and purposes, am a prisoner. Fortunately, dependence implies reciprocity between perspectives. I am dominated and I dominate. I am both bound and free, caught between the pros and the cons. Is that good? Is it right? Is it necessary? I am inclined to say, loudly, that it is.

I adore, in any case, the brevity of this book, which takes flight and soars like an arrow. I can also say, without fear of contradicting myself, that I find it all too short. Sequels are usually reserved for novels.

Paris, 1984

Introduction

I discovered the extraordinary importance of dependence a few years ago in a hospital. I was seriously ill and wasn't allowed to get out of bed or to move at all, even if it was only to go from lying on one side to lying on the other. It was in that state of extreme helplessness that I saw how much a person can be in need of others. I was in need not only of the director of the medical staff and his interns and of the nurses, day and night, but also of the nurses' aides, the masseuse, and the orderlies. Not only for medical care, but for a comforting word or gesture. One night I woke up in considerable pain; since no one dared to make a decision that involved a certain amount of risk, I began to feel as if I were being abandoned. I had to strongly insist before someone finally went to wake up one of the head nurses and then an intern, to get permission to do what was necessary, without which I would have had to put up with almost unbearable pain until the next morning. Observation of my fellow patients was enough to convince me that they were all in the same situation — all, depending on the gravity of their illness, more or less lost, forced to rely on others for their slightest needs. And the only thing they had to look forward to, the only thing that would break up their solitude and give them relief from pain was a visit from their family or from a friend. By the time I left the hospital I had come to the conclusion that dependence is definitely a permanent aspect of life for people who are ill.

Dependence is a specific aspect as well. Having worked for a long time on dominance and subjection [*The Colonizer and the Colonized* and *Dominated Man*], I tried at first to reduce the dependence of the patient to his subjection to the hospital staff, who found in that an opportunity to dominate him. That equivalence soon proved to be insufficient, if not fallacious. It is possible, of course, that those involved in caring for patients get a certain amount of perverse pleasure out of performing their

3

Dependence

duties in an authoritarian manner; but an equally important component of the gratification they get from their work is the satisfaction of knowing that they're indispensable, of *providing* for someone else's needs. The patient may feel as if his need for their help makes him subject to them, but, even more, he expects that help. He asks for it if it's late: he's depending on it in order to get well. In short, I soon realized that I would have to distinguish four kinds of behavior instead of two: subjection and domination on the one hand, dependence and providing on the other. Two diptychs instead of just one, and strongly linked to each other in such a way that they form a unit.

In practice, of course, and in the life of the individual, matters are hardly ever that simple. Those who are dependent get impatient living, as they inevitably do, under the thumb of a provider: adolescents, who are economically and emotionally dependent, find it difficult to tolerate the ambiguity of their parents, who dispense material goods but also anxiously monitor their behavior. It is difficult for a provider to avoid profiting from his own beneficence: parents get pleasure, confidence, and legitimacy out of their devotion. A dominator is sometimes also a donator. Employers sometimes fancy themselves to be philanthropists; some colonizers have acted like protectors of those they've colonized. A dominated person may hope to get subsidies and protection from the person who is dominating. But it is precisely because reality involves such deviations, complexities, and impurities that the conceptual tool has to be as keen and as analytic as possible.

I had already learned from examining the relations between dominators and the dominated that the behavior of those who are subject is not the exact obverse or a simple negative imprint of the behavior of those who dominate. It is, of course, principally a response to an oppressive situation. The stratagems employed by women in their relationships with men and the humor of Jews and of colonized peoples are ways of circumventing or mitigating the effects of the law that gives dominion to those who are strong. More generally, the overall character of the dominated party is determined by that of the dominator. The opposite is true as well: colonized peoples take on the characteristics of those who have colonized them, but colonizers are also influenced by the subject population. Their ways of behaving, certain character traits, and even their respective ideologies are curiously intertwined. Nevertheless, despite these obvious correlations, their portraits aren't superimposable, nor do they even correspond to each other point for point. Each one has its singularity, its dynamism, and its share of unexpected attributes. To be effective, a ruse has to be inventive because its success depends on the element of surprise. In short, the behavior of those who are dominated has a certain specificity with respect to the behavior of those who dominate and it has to be examined separately.

There is a tendency now to equate dependence with subjection, to the advantage of subjection. Saying that a person is dependent is considered just another way of saying that she's dominated. But even a superficial analysis is enough to show that dependence and subjection are not equivalent; although the dependent person and the dominated person are both alienated, they're not alienated in the same way. Although both have, to a certain extent, lost some of their capacity for independent action, the differences between them are greater than the similarities. Essentially, the dependent person more or less consents to her alienation; the dominated person does not. The reason is clear: the dependent person gets something out of being alienated; the dominated person does not. It's possible, of course, to be simultaneously dependent and dominated, but that coincidence is neither automatic nor necessary. *Dependence isn't the same as subjection,* even if they happen to occur together. Nor does the fact that dependence sometimes develops within domination mean that dependence can be reduced to a consequence of domination. I have shown elsewhere how, at a certain point in their journey through life, the colonized imitate and often admire those who have colonized them; but that does not mean that they consent to domination. Such behavior is even a sign of the contrary, of their refusal to give that approbation. If they adopt the ways of those who, because of their dominant position, have become their models, it is because they want to take their place, to end their domination.

Those who are dependent, however, are obviously not looking for ways to terminate their dependency relationships. They find them quite rewarding, as a matter of fact, and they hesitate to think what life would be like without them. Drinkers can't wait to get a drink and smokers can't wait for a chance to smoke; and if they're prevented from doing so, they become miserable and aggressive. Dependent people may be irritated with their providers and become hostile toward them but the dependents still need the providers, and that is the origin of their righteous disappointment. When a person is dependent on someone, he is at that person's mercy. But that means two different things: it means the person hopes to enjoy the provider's good graces and also that the person hopes to gain something from the relationship. ''I need you'' means both ''I'm dependent on you'' and ''I hope to get something from you.'' To be under the domination of someone is to be subordinated to that person without any appreciable gain, unless the dominator is also a provider. Contrary to what people sometimes think, the cohesion that characterizes large social organizations like churches and armies is not based just on authority, hierarchy, and an apparatus of repression. It also comes from a profound allegiance on the part of the members, who benefit a great deal from adherence to such groups.

*

All of this soon seemed to me to be obvious and, I must add, highly convenient. Why hadn't I noticed it earlier? In truth, now that I think of it, I realize that I have often had occasion to describe, even at great length, dependent behavior. But I did not expressly call it that and rarely insisted on its specificity. When I studied the imitation of the dominator by those who are dominated, which is essentially a form of *dependence on a model,* it would have been easy for me to include dependence in the perspective of a more general dominance. I didn't do so; to be more exact, I dealt with it without naming it. Why was I guilty, so to speak, of such negligence? I can think of only one explanation: preoccupied with relationships involving dominance and subjection, and the mechanisms that make them work, I had a tendency to try, as I had done in the hospital, to reduce everything to dominance and subjection. To be more precise, I was bent on reducing everything, for reasons that are obscure and not methodological, which I can now distinguish. I probably was extremely reluctant to acknowledge and to inventory my own dependencies. But there was also another, related, more objective reason. I was painting a picture of oppression in order to condemn and combat it. Perhaps I had the impression, in spite of myself, that if I had introduced a third element into the opposition between dominance and subjection, I would have attenuated the responsibility of those who are dominant. I am quite willing to admit today that, at the age I had attained when I first undertook the task I had assigned myself, I was full of passion, humiliation, resentment against injustice, and impatient hope for changes in the course of things and in my own life.

Dependence

But, as always, I ultimately convinced myself that the truth is more profitable. Far from being diminished by the establishment of dependence as a fact, our understanding of the relationships between dominators and the dominated is increased by this complementary exchange, which gives us a better idea of their complexity and a greater mastery of the subject. It also helps us to better account for one of the most surprising aspects of oppression — its amazing tenacity, between individuals and between groups, between the members of a couple, between employers and employees, between nations. And it has this tenacity despite the dissatisfaction, refusals, and rebellions, more or less serious, of those who are being dominated. Strength, fear, mystification, and illusions don't explain everything.

I offer two more examples. During the last few decades we have seen two very significant and welcome developments: the transformation of the status of women and decolonization, that is, the end of feminine subjection and the advent of national independence for numerous races of people. I have applauded and continue to applaud, almost without reservation, these liberations. I do not, nevertheless, think it is vain or scandalous to say that the relative stability of the married couple cannot be explained simply in terms of the yoke imposed on the woman by the man, or even in terms of a reciprocal yoke, without reference to the reciprocal *need* experienced by the two partners. If we did not take this need into account, it would be impossible to understand a great deal of what sometimes appears to be aberrant behavior on the part of both men and women. In an amorous relationship, the dominant person isn't always the least dependent one. The authors of literary works have been suggesting this to us for quite some time through many of their characters: the unfortunate Othello and the Chevalier des Grieux are prisoners of their passion just as much as Anna Karenina and the heroine of *The Story of O*, who allowed herself to be tortured. This in no way diminishes, of course, the gravity of the historical harm that has been done to women or the debt owed to women by men.

When we look at the relationships that exist today between nations that were formerly on opposite ends of a particular colonial adventure, we have every right to be surprised. We would expect to find all ties between such nations completely broken, but what we see are new ties being formed. This would be good news except that, all too often, the former colonial power has maintained its supremacy. It is easy to see why the former masters contrive to hold on to their position, but why do their former subjects let them do it? Why do people who have waited so long for their autonomy, and have often paid so dearly for it, give up even a part of it? They're obviously compelled to do so. But how? Once they become independent, they have in their own fashion all the trappings of national sovereignty, including political power and its administrative and military instruments. Their compulsion is different from the kind they had to deal with before. We can only conclude that some former colonies find it advantageous, as far as subsistence, security, or their need for technology is concerned, to enter into renewed commerce with their former masters.

We may consider the price they pay for what they get excessive or demeaning; and it may be that, by entering into such arrangements, they are relying on others when they should be concentrating on what they can do for themselves. We may suspect the ruling classes of getting more out of the new situation than the rest of the population. But there is not always dissension between those in power and the rest of the people on that point, so we can assume that the arrangement is acceptable to all concerned and that many former colonial subjects prefer relative dependence to complete independence. Before we cast the first stone we should bear in mind that many nations that have been established for centuries and are more developed are also content, despite their proud proclamations and their resentment of the major powers, to be dependent economically, militarily, and even culturally. In any case, if the end of colonization is the end of subjection, it is not always the end of dependence. As for the relationships between men and women, we may be making a transition from subjection to reciprocal and voluntary dependence.

Clearly there is more to all this than just dominance and subjection; there is also consent, connivance, and dependence. Women who have maids know how dependent they are on such people, even though they can order them about and dismiss them at any time. Is anyone *forcing* the younger generation in Europe to wear jeans and listen to American music day and night? Did anyone force their prewar counterparts to wear high-necked Russian shirts? Who gave the order that started the recent trend of wearing Mao jackets? What is the origin of such cultural fascinations?

Domination does not explain everything, even if it does almost always play a role in most human relationships and even if we are constantly obliged to resist the influence of those who are powerful. The behavior of individuals and groups today is an indissoluble mixture of dependence and subjection, dominance and providing. Moralists and politicans may bemoan the fact and warn us about the voracity of those who are dominant, about the price they exact for their poisoned gifts. But they will never prevent individuals and nations who are in need from becoming more or less dependent on those who can provide for them. This in turn makes the strong even stronger. Does anyone today refuse to profit by the scientific and technological knowledge acquired by the Americans, the Russians, and the Japanese? Does anyone totally neglect the flowering of culture that accompanies the development of modern empires? In short, no study of dominance would be complete that ignored the dependent behavior that goes with dominance.

More generally, every human being needs other human beings to survive. So each person has positive feelings of attraction toward others because each person finds herself in situations involving dependence with respect to others. She finds herself, however, no less frequently in conflict with them. To survive, she has to appropriate certain goods that others also covet or to protect herself against their attempts to appropriate things for themselves. So she has feelings of repulsion and hostility toward them; this constant struggle is the force that keeps the mechanisms of domination in motion. It is a clear case of two competing and complementary impulses serving the same purpose.

This business of dependence has become especially important to me as a way of understanding myself and my relationships with other people and as a way of understanding other people, both individuals and groups. It is also definitely important for the interpretation of cultural works, which are the symbolic yet most enlightening expression of human obsessions, schemes, and behavior. When I approach someone for the first time, I don't wonder just if he is single or married, if he has children, what he does for a living or for recreation, what he thinks about economics, politics, culture, philosophy, or religion, what is dominating and influencing him, and whom he might be dominating and manipulating to his advantage. I now also want to know about his dependencies: on whom and on what is he dependent and who or what is dependent on him — in short, what network of dependencies encompasses and supports his existence. I know what binds me permanently to a few people and a few groups, to whom or to which I belong by birth or

Dependence

adoption. When I examine the profile or the fate of a people, I am no longer content to just bring to light, as I have done in the past, all the relationships involving dominance and subjection that mark the group and its connections with other societies. I try to uncover the tissue of dependencies that orients its sensitivity, its behavior, and its consciousness of itself. When I read a book or go to a play, I always try to find out what forms of dependence the author has used, more or less consciously, to construct the work. Racine has given us good reason to think that each of his characters, every one of whom was all-powerful by virtue of his or her influence on someone else, was wretchedly dependent on a third person. *Andromaque* is the exposition of a chain of dependencies: one must simply know how to read it.

I've convinced myself and I try to convince others of the richness, complexity, and diversity of this other type of human relationship. I am thoroughly persuaded that dependence is both a fact of life so common that it is almost a part of the individual and collective psyche and an operational concept so efficacious that it furnishes an invaluable key to the understanding of people and groups and of their various works, forms of expression, and patterns of behavior. I am so certain about this that I would find it very difficult if I had to decide which of the two combinations — subjection and dominance or dependence and providing — is more important.* I will just say that I think the forms of dependence exhibit as much variety and originality as those of subjection or domination and that I consider it impossible to make an approach to the reality of human existence without systematically taking them into account.

I am convinced that the proper answer to the question "Who is dependent" is "Everyone" — everyone in his or her own way,

---

*See the appendix for a full definition of dependence and other key words.

of course, to a different degree, on one or several objects, and in a manner that is dynamic and variable according to the circumstances. But the portrait of the dependent person sketched here could, after being judiciously retouched to suit the particular case, be that of anyone. The dependent person is still one of the most common and most indisputable images of universal humanity as common and as indisputable as the image of the person who dominates or is dominated. Often it is the same image seen under a different light, for if people frequently dominate one another, they at least as frequently have need of one another.

I

The Dependent and the Provider

Is there anyone who has never seen a panic-stricken child, lost among the crowd in a department store, crying for Mama and no one else, refusing to be consoled by anything — kind words, candy, toys — and whose despair miraculously vanishes as soon as Mama appears? Is there anyone who does not know a married person who gets "worried to death" when his or her spouse is the least bit late and whose anxiety disappears abruptly when the absent partner returns, if it doesn't change to sudden anger? In the marital relationship, as in the parental, the mere presence of the other person can be protection against distress.

In other cases an apparently insignificant object seems so important to certain dependents that it does not seem to matter who procures the object for them. There is, as everyone knows, a sort of camaraderie among smokers; a smoker will accept a cigarette even from an enemy and offer tobacco even to someone she hates. She doesn't care at all about the background of her supplier; it's the supply that counts.

But those are extreme examples. It does happen that the provider and the object provided coincide because one overshadows the other. The child who sucks his thumb seems to prefer that to anything else in the universe; a teddy bear given to a child by his parents seems to replace the parents quite well. But, ordinarily, there are three elements that come together to establish an equation of dependence: the person who hopes to gain something from it; the object the person covets; and the person who procures the object. It is best to remember that dependence is a trinitarian relationship: two partners and an object. I will call them, respectively, the dependent, the provider, and the object provided.* And it will always be instructive to ask three

---

*This trinitarian relationship could be illustrated by taking as a model a triangle, whose points would represent the dependent, the provider, and the object provided.

Dependence

questions: *Who* is dependent? On *whom?* And *for what?*

It is obvious that the way in which one is dependent varies according to whether one is a child, an adolescent, an adult, or an elderly person, a man or a woman. The experiences and social roles, and thus relations with other people, are not the same. Dependence also varies according to whether one is dependent on a living being, human or animal, on an individual or on a group, on a concrete object or on an entity. Attaching oneself to a woman is not the same as attaching oneself to a man or to a dog, to a political party or to a divinity. The quality of the bonds and the rituals that they impose are appreciably different. Finally, the way in which one is dependent varies according to the different objects provided. Collecting lovers is not the same as collecting medals or butterflies; drinking is not the same as smoking; drinking wine is not the same as drinking beer or liquor; smoking ordinary tobacco is not the same as smoking hashish or ingesting hard drugs — they are not all equally toxic or addictive.

So dependence can be viewed from three perspectives: according to the identity of the dependent, to that of the provider, and to the object provided. I will restrict myself to the point of view of the dependent, whose portrait is the principal purpose of this book. It would be useless in any case to attempt to make an exhaustive list of objects provided: they are innumerable. I will mention them only insofar as they shed light on the personality of the dependent. If I dwell a bit more on the provider, however, I will not try to offer a direct and complete picture of him or her; I will confine myself to those traits that can help us to better understand the dependent.

In conclusion, an equation of dependence is not immutable. Passions sometimes do not last any longer than bursts of flame; the flames change into embers and the embers into ashes. Despite the wishes of the dependent, providers come and go, or they change; objects provided are used up or deteriorate. And, most of all, as the years go by, the dependent himself or herself is no longer the same. A bereavement, a separation, or a new acquaintance, a change in one's situation with respect to family or friends, societal events that are either depressing or exciting, an alteration or shock in one's psychic universe — the profile of the dependent is subject to some surprising modifications. Her old habits become almost foreign to her, and she contracts new ones; it is as if she had assumed a new identity and started a new life. The gambler who used to spend his days and nights at the casino is now so changed that his old way of life is just an amusing memory; the inveterate drinker firmly refuses the smallest drop of alcohol. On the other hand, dependents are sometimes transformed into devout militants or zealous believers. In short, like that of the dominated, the portrait of the dependent is clearly dynamic.

I will try, nevertheless, to single out the principal characteristics, the most frequent and most stable, from which all the others can be deduced.

The Duet

The general characteristics of a particular dependent will undoubtedly be determined by those of his or her provider. Like parent, like child; but also like child, like parent; and even like husband, like wife and the converse. The manner in which the provider herself, provides the manner in which she considers her exigent partner — with favor, annoyance, or revolt — and the manner, good or bad, in which she responds to her partner's demands have their effect on the dependent.

On the other hand, the behavior of the provider is not entirely unrelated to that of the dependent. Every child is, of course,

Dependence

the child of a given mother, but every child marks the birth of a certain mother. If the ability or inability of the mother to express her emotions influences the development of her child, then the character of the child and the ease or difficulty with which he adapts to life have more than a little to do with the fate of the mother. "When I substitute for one of my colleagues," confides a doctor, "I can draw a picture of him from my observation of his patients." Every doctor eventually gathers around him patients who suit him, as much as he suits them. A person suffering from anxiety looks not for a doctor who is overcalm but for an interlocutor capable, by virtue of intuition or experience, of dealing with her fears. A bit of personal anxiety on the part of the therapist does not make him unfit to treat patients suffering from anxiety, to whom a certain dramatization of their case gives the impression of being taken seriously.

What we find is a *duet.* I have already written about this notion [in *Dominated Man*], about its fecundity and methodological interest, so it is unnecessary to dwell on it again at any length. Colonizer-colonized, man-woman, white-black, master-domestic — provider-dependent. It seems to be impossible today to think of anyone at all except in terms of such relationships. Each partner in the inevitable duet is transformed by it in conduct and thought. In addition, each of us is involved in several duets. Who will not agree, moreover, that we don't play the same role in each of them? A married woman thought to be very dull can show herself to be unexpectedly amusing when away from her husband. We don't even play the same role in the presence of the same partner in public or in private, for example. The time, the situation, the code imposed on us by our circumstances and surroundings all have something to do with the quality of the dialogue, the intensity of each voice, and the amplitude of the echo.

The Dependent and the Provider

Images of the Provider

It may seem necessary, because of this diversity, to try to reduce all the images of the provider to one: that of the mother or, rather, the mother-father, a mythical, nurturing, loving, caring and protective entity. All forms of dependence would then be continuations of infantile dependence, at best a flowering of multiple roles on a single stem. Pressed by various demands, we distribute ourselves differently according to the appeals; but it would always be a case of the same response, of the same effort to reestablish a few fundamental equilibriums.

There is an important genetic truth here: everything begins with the child and, for that reason, the parent-child relationship will continue to be privileged. Some people spend their whole lives at that stage; we all retain for it a persistent nostalgia that cuts across the ties, of varying degrees of certainty and permanence, that we incessantly try to form. This fundamental duet in one way or another will always be a part of human existence. That is why the couple is for almost all of us the great duet: it is so strongly reminiscent of the other. That is why love is the most constant theme of all the artistic productions of every era. Romantic love curiously evokes the most primitive kind of exclusivism, that of the child, which is a mixture of the utmost happiness and the cruelest anguish — the fear of separation. It is well known that the progeny of humans are particularly eager for care and attention because of their total impotence at birth, the duration of their nursing period, and the length of their adolescence. Adults will never completely rid themselves of this uneasy exigence, as if their survival always depended on it.

Nevertheless, these meanderings of the same river all together constitute the reality of human life. A patient investigation of them is necessary for an understanding of the diverse totality of human behaviors. Even if the analysis were to continually

Dependence

lead to the child that persists in us, to the Oedipus complex, to nothing but the desire for economic gain, or to a few impulses, it has been a long time since we were just that child. What constitutes us now are all those chains of mediations, new interests, personal experiences, hopes, and limitations, and even our pretensions and illusions. Those things are what make us the men and women we have become. The daily life of an adult involves many images of the provider. It is important to distinguish them and to describe them separately.

The most common image next to that of the parental relationship is that of a human partner. We have constructed ourselves starting from that dialogue and we function best under those conditions. We are not autonomous entities who by chance encounter other solitary beings. We exist in relation to other people. We are constantly soliciting their friendship or starting quarrels with them, often to obtain the same result — an exchange and an acknowledgment. And since other people necessarily disappoint us, we try to correct our ideas of them, we reinvent them according to our needs. This process gives us the extraordinary mixture of exact intuitions and fanciful reveries that we have about one another. But when everything else has failed, driven by our excessive and uncontrollable need for others, we look for replacements: subhumans or superhumans with whom we would have the same privileged relationship, improved or intensified.

The gods of antiquity were often absurdly human. Contemporary believers, it is true, maintain that their particular god is totally original. Perhaps. One could also argue that monotheism makes the divinity even more human. There is no doubt about it in the case of Christ, an emanation and replica of God and, at the same time, an advocate for men and women before the Eternal Father. Muhammad is even more clearly an intercessor. The god of the Jews didn't even need an intermediary: he communicated with his people directly in an I-thou that was often quite blunt. The single god is more efficacious for dependence because of a unique and personal relationship with the believer.

The relationship with the divinity is not the only one that reveals something about the individual or collective soul. All those bizarre creatures who abound in the history of peoples — genies, fairies, ogres, djinns, emanations from the ground, air, fire, forests, rivers, and mountains, demons, and devils — are essentially different sorts of humans, more benevolent or more malevolent. Their specific powers are not entirely fantastic: they are amplifications of the potentialities of real men and women; they are simply out of the ordinary. The worship of the dead, the practices of magic, and the rituals of possession and exorcism teach us a great deal about ourselves. The actions of those who are possessed are not completely without rhyme or reason. Such people conform to an internalized model. Recent psychiatric cases and certain ethnographic films by the French film maker Jean Rouch have taught us that the frenzies of the colonized have some significance: they express their ambiguous conflicts with the colonizer.

Reciprocal Dependence

In truth, everything teaches us about ourselves because everything we do is a form of self-expression. How could we possibly fail to discover important facts about ourselves in a relationship as persistent as dependence — in the way we drive a car, smoke, drink, or eat, and, especially, in the way we treat other people or in what we expect of others? That is to say in those constant *reciprocal dependencies* that define and restrict the compass of our lives.

Dependence on animals, and the reciprocal dependence of animals on humans, goes back to the beginning of time. The domestication of certain species has made them our inseparable

Dependence

companions. It is an association in which each partner counts
on the other for survival or comfort, in which each is simultaneously the dependent of and provider for the other. A horse is
just as dependent on its rider as the rider is on the horse: it is
fed, cared for, and protected by its master. An unshod horse
often ends up dying. Wounded and crippled, it can no longer
escape from larger animals; it can't get to new pastures and sometimes starves to death. A rider, thanks to her mount, can better
protect herself from her enemies or the rigors of a local climate.
That is why horse thieves used to be hung: without a mount,
a person was in mortal danger. In short, the rider and the horse
find in their alliance the same benefit — a victory over space.
A nomad's dog helps with the hunting and protects the area
around the tent. Although most of our lives are now more
sedentary and dogs are bred, this dual function persists, more
or less symbolically, in the use of dogs to guard our homes and
to accompany us on weekend hunts. Other needs, no doubt, are
also satisfied by this coexistence with animals who have become
so familiar that they are almost familial. There are approximately
ten million pets in France. Obviously they are kept not for
guarding our apartments or because they are fashionable, but
because people want some living thing in their midst. Hasn't
everyone at one time seen an older person out all alone walking
a dog? How many couples, as soon as their children leave the
house, start to raise a dog or a cat, prolonging, surprisingly, the
duties and problems of parenthood and the cares, worries about
subsistence, and limitations on their freedom of movement that
they seemed eager to put out of their lives?

Resemblance and Specificity

We may laugh at the idea of having such affection for an
animal; we may try to explain it in terms of something else. The

24

dog, we might say, probably correctly, takes the place of the son or daughter who has gone away; a hamster for an only child replaces the sibling he or she doesn't have. But this interpretation, even if correct, doesn't exhaust the specificity of a course of conduct. A child will weep, really weep, if his cat gets sick (the cat and not his little sister, who has never existed); his parents will do everything possible to cure the animal, and its death will be a minor tragedy for the whole family. A number of writers have devoted books to the story of their attachment to an animal. In addition to Jack London and others, François Nourissier, Jules Roy, and Colette Audry have described such experiences with great sincerity. Audry, a strong, politically militant woman who is as far as possible from a "mommy with a little doggie," at first resisted this kind of affection. Prevailed upon by her son to adopt a little female dog, Douchka, she readily admits that she contemplated, and even tried, getting rid of it. Nothing worked: irresistibly — the word is not too strong for anyone who has read her account — a reciprocal dependence developed between her and Douchka and between Douchka and her son. And when the dog got sick and died, the author felt bereaved and wept, as if she were mourning for a person she loved. It is equally apparent from these books that the dependence of the animal is just as strong. A lost dog will always come back, often from a considerable distance; a dog won't sleep if its masters are awake, and it sleeps when they sleep. A dog is the dog of a particular master, just as a child is the child of particular parents. The ability of an animal to anticipate is no less remarkable than that of humans. Animals have the capacity for thought and emotion; experts have demonstrated this, but those who have lived with animals have always been sure of it. A cow feels real pain when her offspring are taken from her, and who can say that she doesn't have any thoughts before the frightful event.

Dependence

Whether it be a need for tenderness, a cure for solitude, a desire for contact with nature, identification with an animal, or perhaps motives that are not so commendable — an outlet for a tendency to dominate, the possibility of fashioning a living thing to one's own image of which one can be proud — it makes no difference: dependence on an animal is a bond that is rich and complex. It is simultaneously close to and different from that which links the child to his or her parents. The animal is an adult that will not necessarily die if it is abandoned; the identification is, in spite of everything, not complete. From another point of view, the manifestations of animal dependence and providing are different from those of an adult human being because of language and the special nature of human socialization.

Dependence on an Object

Dependence on an object involves an even more difficult problem: how can one attach oneself, directly, to an object? Should we still speak of dependence? Isn't it rather a detour, ruse, or last resort, a substitute for a real duet, that is, a duet with a living being? The object would in that case be related to a provider, who would, for some reason, be hidden.

There would be no lack of arguments for such an interpretation. Drivers become infatuated with their automobiles. It is symptomatic that they need to compare them to living things, for example to women. They say that they "take care" of their cars, "spoil" them, so that they won't "desert" them; they are proud of them. All the same, such associations remain in the realm of analogy; most people would agree about that, with a smile. A car is an object, which they treat as such and with which they part without regret, in favor of one that is newer.

The difficulty is diminished considerably if we focus on the dependent rather than on the object provided. Everything happens as if there existed a floating dependence that comes to rest on a more or less interchangeable support. This support can be a living creature, human or animal; it can be an inanimate object. It isn't necessary to assume that the car has replaced some parent figure. It is more likely that the car has taken the place of the horse. More or less unconsciously, we have made it into a symbol of the same important things: security in particular. That is why people react so violently when other people touch their cars: without them they would be immobilized — they couldn't get away. The fact that a car is a closed space is not without significance — it is a little house, a shelter. We can explain to a smoker that a cigarette is a substitute for a breast, that he is nursing on his pipe or cigar. If he's in a good mood, he'll agree, but that reference to a distant past hardly interests him and won't change his behavior at all. He just wants to smoke.

Dependence on an object, while it may be just a stop along the way for the dependent, is unique in several respects, and it would be an error, a waste, if we didn't consider the riches of this aspect of dependence. It is almost the only aspect that affords us an experimental perspective; we can in many cases observe and even produce variations in the object provided. The smoker knows the number of cigarettes he needs every day and the drinker knows approximately how much alcohol she drinks; they both know what circumstances will make them consume more or less. They can see for themselves the psychic and physiological modifications that result from the absorption or non-absorption of their favorite drugs. It is therefore possible to correlate, or even quantify, the elements of such a dependence.

Because we can measure one of the variables, it is possible to arrive at objective descriptions; that isn't easy in a study of jealousy or envy. In this respect, the most common kind of

Dependence

dependence proves to be remarkably complex. Inhaling smoke is a form of toxicomania, to be sure, but the act of smoking in its entirety serves many purposes: the suction, the pleasant contact with the lips and the mucous membranes of the mouth, the ingestion, so reminiscent of the comforting and promising act of taking nourishment, and then the whole dance with the hands — the filling of the pipe, the rolling of the cigarette, the preparation of the cigar, the endless manipulation of matches or lighter occupy both the body and the mind, just as knitting or weaving does. Manual labor has a calming effect in that it takes a person's thoughts off herself and provides an outlet for her nervous energy. Mountain climbers often describe the extraordinary euphoria they experience while climbing and how they are disturbed to think that they will someday be unable to climb. Hunters do not always, economically, need what they catch. Hunting is a labor of love. "When the seals are out there and I can't go," one hunter admits, "it makes me physically ill." The nervous system is in fact provided with a means of expunging the excess of unemployed activity. Even chewing gum, which we keep in our mouths long after its sugar is gone, or the gum arabic of my youth, which didn't even have sugar and which we would sometimes replace with rubber washers salvaged from lemonade bottles, serves the same purpose.

These simple adaptations are related to rituals. We are far from having heard the final word on the subject of rituals. We are witnessing the increasing success of pharmacology. Some people have to take a sedative every night; others always carry tranquilizers. But how much of this is the chemical influence and how much is ritual? Taking medicine is often an echo of the medical prescription, an invocation of the person of the doctor, in the same way that touching an amulet or holy image reminds a person of a spirit or a saint (this brings up the third

28

element of the trinitarian equation — a hidden provider). A ritual is a permanent exorcism against some anxiety or possible threat from without. Smoking is clearly an individual and social ritual, a mannerism, a way of giving assurance, and a means of communication, if not of communion, of struggling against solitude. Drug addicts speak significantly of "joints"; smokers willingly offer their cigarettes or tobacco pouches; and drinkers never refuse a drink, for it would be antisocial, almost an offense. The activities of high society are in effect interindividual occupations. They postulate and consolidate society at large.

Rituals are ultimately connected to ideologies. Smoking and drinking are also collective behaviors governed by values. Conversely, an ideology derives support and reinforcement from the rituals that express it. The rosary is, simultaneously, an object that calms the nerves (the Greeks use a secular rosary, the *komboloi,* that they constantly finger), an ingredient of a social ritual, and its sign. The member of the faithful who runs a set of wooden or amber beads through her fingers until they are worn to dust, like the priest who reads and reads his breviary, gets from this activity personal, nervous, and psychic rewards and reaffirms at the same time a cultural and religious tradition. The increasing number of women who are starting to smoke are not doing so just to experience the effects of nicotine: they want, more or less consciously, to perform a masculine ritual.

The Collective Provider

An object provided is anything that makes it possible for a person to respond to a dependence — a being, an object in the strict sense of the word, a representation, or an activity. What else can we call the extraordinary connection between so many people and their work if not a dependence-providing relationship? It is sufficient to see such people, as soon as they are out

Dependence

of work, contrive to find some sort of occupation, as if they had to reproduce at any cost their temporarily suspended professional duties. Miners are said to be and to call themselves "slaves of the mine." The phrase is relatively accurate, but there is reason to believe that the expression is ambiguous — simultaneously they are prisoners and are proud of their social utility, traditions, and virtues of courage and tenacity. The curse of work is also a blessing; it is the ambiguity of all dependence.

A film on television one night told the story of a businessman who owns a factory that his father had started and he has developed. Business is bad, so he has to sell his shares to a group of foreigners. He meets a callgirl, a child of poverty who hates men and treats them worse than dogs. Contrary to all expectations, this captain of industry, until then a strong man who had succeeded in making his family business into an international enterprise, falls in love with the prostitute and puts up with the worst treatment from her. The director of the film seemed surprised himself at this "respectable man in love with a whore" and was visibly trying to convey his astonishment to the viewer.

But the schema of dependence gives us the key to the romantic mystery of the human heart. What we witness in this film is just a passage from dependence on one thing to dependence on another. The hero, precisely because he was very much dependent on his business, does not know what to do without it; he breaks down and attaches himself to the first woman who comes along. The same film contains the counterpoint to this dependence on a profession. The factory workers are just as disoriented as their boss by the change in their status. When they learn that he has decided to give up control of the business, they react violently. They turn on the hero and accuse him of treachery, even though they love him and he loves them, in part because of that affection. Stripped of the romantic dimension, their dependence is even more obvious; they, also, are attached to the factory, to which they are tributaries in both senses: dominated and dependent, like many workers. When people say about their work — be it in a factory, service, store, or office — "It's all I live for," they also mean to suggest, "It's all that's keeping me alive."

Here we encounter another difficulty: by a tacit agreement, which conceals the confusion in our thinking, we talk about collective entities as if they were single individuals having a life comparable to that of humans or animals. But this assimilation is metaphorical, if not erroneous. What exactly is a collective conscience or memory, or even a collective endeavor? When we speak of "the body of society" we are obviously not referring to an aggregation of physiological processes governed by a nervous system and expressing itself in psychic manifestations. Even when we speak of conduct, of collective behavior, that can be described from without, are the phenomena really essentially the same as individual forms of conduct and behavior? Someday we will definitely have to develop a more adequate vocabulary for the "life" of groups. And someday, provided that we are more enlightened about that life, perhaps we will understand what it means for a group to be devoted to a person or for a person to sacrifice himself or herself for a group.

In the meantime, and with the reservations I have already mentioned, if we assume that a factory, an organization, or a social group is a collective being, we can safely say that there exist collective dependencies and collective forms of providing — dependence of a group on a group, dependence of a group on an individual, and vice versa.

We can try to reduce these entities to the image of a mother or father. Evidence to support such inferences is found in certain terms we use: "the fatherland" or "the mother country"; "our

Dependence

mother the Church,'' with its corollaries and relatives; her ''eldest daughter'' France, whose claim to this title is, however, disputed. A university is, at least for those who teach there, an *alma mater* — see how many mothers we seek to provide for ourselves — the army, political parties, and athletic teams are all ''big families''; and even espionage agencies are, for their employees, ''the family.'' All of this is half jest and half conviction, but it leads in every instance to typical forms of behavior, each of which warrants attention. The proof that such dependencies indeed exist is that a breach with a ''collective being'' is often traumatic, as painful as a separation from an individual. The priest who abandons his order or the militant who does not renew his card feels that ''life no longer makes any sense,'' unless he has already found something else. The group, for its part, condemns those who leave it as renegades who deserve violent treatment.

The truth is that a group is more than a group. It is an institution and a network of institutions, which support and protect the lives of their members. It is the repository of the common values that orient and guide the conduct of its members. Although the group seems to act in its own interests, often with self-centered cruelty, even against the individuals of which it is composed, we vaguely admit that in serving the group we serve ourselves. In defending itself, even against each of us, the group indirectly defends us. So the legitimacy of the group resides, ultimately, in the constant approbation of each member. Without that continued unanimous adherence, the group would start to disintegrate.

This is obvious in the case of those groupings — country clubs, athletic associations, or trade organizations — that are perpetuated by the free will of those who participate. It is also true for those institutions that seem to defy the passage of time, that the individual finds in existence when he is born and that he can't rebel against without serious consequences. The educational system of a nation is continuously consolidated and revitalized by the active respect of each citizen. In short, it is the dependent who confirms the different images of the provider.

Dependence on Values

It isn't easy to distinguish dependence on a group, dependence on institutions, and dependence on values. How could we have any serious concept of Christianity that didn't include the collective body of Christians? Any idea of a doctrine apart from its historical applications? To defend a set of values is to be a part, in some way, of the group that embodies those values. To be dependent on a group is always to adhere, to a certain extent, to its institutions and values which in return furnish a justification and a guarantee for that dependence. Once again, the distinction is not without utility.

Certain Christians like to proclaim that one should not confuse the Church with Christianity. They would consent to die, they say, for the teachings of Christ, but not for the changes introduced by the clerical organization and the designs of its hierarchy. Certain political militants explain their party affiliation strictly in terms of a moral choice. The errors, or even crimes, commited by those who compose the party are, according to the militants, negligible compared to their ideal of justice and progress. Regardless of whether their attitude has any foundation in law, it is the inspiration for their conduct. Militants can find themselves in conflict with their associates in the very name of the values they have in common. Sometimes Christians refuse to submit to their Church in the name of Christian values: the French integrists, led by Archbishop Lefebvre, are the most recent example. Our distant revolt against French colonization was staged in the name of French values.

Dependence

In *Death in Venice,* Thomas Mann describes the conflict between art and life in the creative person. His hero, completely dedicated to literature, is recalled to life by his homosexual passion for a boy. For a time he thinks he can sublimate his attraction in a Platonic love for the beauty of the young man, that is, in maintaining his customary aesthetic attitude. He fails to do so and has to face the facts: his desires are going to get the better of him. He is saved from this fate only by the opportune intervention of a *deus ex machina*: he dies in an epidemic. But that ending is not as artificial as it might seem. Mann may be suggesting that the conflict is insoluble. As soon as the artist allows himself to get caught up in life, he is lost to art: it is art or life. Worse still, since he makes his living exclusively from art, there is nothing left for him but to die physically. He does not really have a choice between spiritual or physical death because spiritual renunciation will lead to his destruction. The artist does not have the right to the satisfactions granted to ordinary mortals — it is always art against life.

Hence the revolt of Faust, which is a rebellion against spiritual dependence. In Goethe's version, life triumphs over knowledge. Because he discovers in the twilight of his life that he hasn't really lived, Faust repudiates the values of scholarship. He agrees to trade his soul for a second youth and the pleasures of that age. Unlike the hero of *Death in Venice,* Faust experiences no regrets and manages, through a subterfuge, to recover his soul. The conflict is thus resolved in favor of life. The same thing happens in the novel *Gradiva,* by Jensen, which had the good fortune, historically, to serve as a preliminary sketch for the ideas of Freud. The hero, Norbert Hanold, driven to complete distraction by his passion for ethnology, no longer notices his pretty female neighbor, with whom he is unknowingly in love and who is in love with him. Neglecting the real woman, he has eyes only for statues, to the point of risking his mental equilibrium for them. With the help of the young woman, he eventually begins to recover, that is, to live. The story captured the imagination of Freud.

The route taken by Leonardo da Vinci presents a happy balance between two types of values — art and knowledge — expressed at certain times by pictorial works and at others by research into problems of engineering.

The Reality and Ideality of the Provider

Dependence on values is essentially a particular case of a very broad category: dependence on symbolic objects. Symbolism is everywhere, at least for human beings. A group is perceived as an object, a collective body, and an institution and, simultaneously, as an aggregation of symbols. An indivual is a symbol as well. The passage from the individual to the collective is effected as an enlargement of the symbolic sphere. The experience of human social organization begins with symbolism — assuming that animals have no intuition of symbols. The human individual is precociously imbued with symbols because parental relations are governed by the numerous codes common to all social life.

In other words, the provider is always more or less ideal, by which I mean constructed or imagined by the mind. People who are dependent are clearly more concerned about their relationship with the provider than they are with the provider's real character. The provider is always, to a certain extent, a figment of the dependent's imagination, because the dependent's perception of the provider is influenced by the dependent's own expectations.

In the therapeutic relationship, what is the role of the real doctor and that of the ideal doctor? Of the physical and social person of the therapist and of the idea one has of him or her, even in advance of a first meeting? The current image of the therapist is a mixture of various stereotypes: the old mythical figure of the sorcerer-healer, possessor of magic powers, authority on beneficial potions and rituals and at the same time the figure of the modern scientist, the engineer with efficacious methods, dispenser of lifesaving remedies. One image succeeds the other, the two blending despite the difference in their historical ages.

In the dependence of a child on a parent, of a child on an older brother or sister, of an apprentice on his master, and, in a general way, of those who have the least on those who have the most, there is a dependence on a model as much as on a real person. That is the origin of the doubt and ambiguity that inevitably mark all dependence and inevitably give birth to disappointment and resentment.

What is the role of the real and of the ideal construction in romantic behavior? It is discovered too late, at the moment of truth, when the dependence ends or abates: "How could I have seen him or her like that?" In *Swann's Way* Marcel Proust describes quite accurately the way romantic passion waxes and wanes. When the lover comes to see things as they really are, he doesn't understand what has happened to him because his idealized conception of the other person has vanished. A mother or single woman will sometimes continue to carefully lay out clothes, make the bed, and set the table for a deceased child or departed lover who was formerly the source of maternal or romantic satisfactions. It is not unusual to hear of parents who, having lost a child, bring up the next one in the image of the first, going so far in their obsessive fidelity to the deceased as to treat a son like a daughter and vice versa. The unfortunate younger child ends up conforming spontaneously to the model imposed on her, sometimes with doubts about her own nature. Parents and children find themselves in effect tributaries to a being who thereupon becomes ideal.

The Dependent and the Provider

To the question "Why is a person dependent?" we can reply, "Because he believes he is." A dependent is anyone who believes in the efficacity of his provider. A person is in love as long as he believes he is in love. An alcoholic is anyone who believes he can't do without alcohol. In the case of the religious person there is redundance: a believer is anyone who has faith in God. This is obviously insufficient to explain such imperious necessities, but dependence is assuredly, among other things, a matter of belief.

The Imaginary Provider

In extreme cases, the provider can be fictional. That shouldn't be surprising. The human universe being also a world of signs, the signs eventually acquire a relative autonomy. Humans are the only (?) animals capable of indulging in the amazing activity that consists of sitting around in a circle to talk for hours, that is, of playing with words. What is a conversation if not a game of Ping-Pong with ideas instead of balls, played for stakes that are principally in the realm of ideas? One of the most peculiar things about the human mind is its propensity to endow metaphors with life.

We are back to the problem of belief, one of the most troublesome in general psychology. In that quasi creation, in which there can be considerable active complicity on the part of the dependent, what is the role of positive belief? The answer is obvious: the expectations of the dependent are the foundation of his belief in the reality of the provider. If the dependent could clearly see the fictional nature of her provider, she would cease to count on the provider. She would have to find another provider or stop being dependent, at least in theory. In practice, each person chooses the solution that suits her, doubting and believing in proportions that vary according to her mood and the circum-

Dependence

stances. We all live, Shakespeare remarked, in the shadow of a dream; to which we might add, and even of several.

This is plain to see in dependence on art. The author and the reader pretend to consider a fictional universe as if it were veridical. For at least the time it takes to read a work of fiction, the plot is lived almost as if it were real and its characters alive; at the end the reader might have to give himself a vigorous shake to make sure he isn't still musing about it. Sometimes the magic of language or imagery causes hallucinations. Everyone has heard the famous anecdote about Balzac demanding on his deathbed to see the doctor he had created in *The Human Comedy;* or the anecdote about the reader of Alexandre Dumas who rushed over to threaten the author at home because he couldn't stand to wait for the next day's paper to find out what was going to happen to the hero.

In the case of dependence on the sacred, belief is even more complete and more tenacious because more anxiety is attached to the expectations. In a little church in my neighborhood there is an inscription in gold that stands out in the shadowy light: "Without me you can do nothing." Those are the words of Jesus Christ, reported by St. John. Later the saying became "Without the Church there is no salvation." This represents a transition from dependence on an individual to dependence on an institution, the institution being an indirect means of strengthening the tie to the divinity. Without this tie, without the love of God, nothing can be done; with it, hope has no limits. With the stakes so high, it is understandable that the believer should have no desire to question the reality of her God. And if, despite herself, doubts begin to arise, she will do her best to behave exactly as she always had before. She will act as if that possibly fictional being were living and, moreover, infinitely good, more powerful and more intelligent than a human being, because she expects more of God — help of every kind and the promise of immortality, which no mere mortal could ever guarantee. A believer is a person who, having a need to believe, will believe regardless of the arguments against it. Believers, who have written candidly on this subject, agree: they don't conceal their fleeting episodes of confusion or their obstinacy in continuing to believe. They just could not tolerate, if they doubted, the dangerous confusion what would enter their lives. Many non-believers recognize, moreover, that the divinity is an extraordinarily effective spiritual construct. If so many multitudes have created and re-created it, it is because they were fervently calling for it with their prayers. Religion may not have the legitimacy of truth, but it does have the legitimacy of need.

Many others, who have abandoned religion, have sought a similar kind of help from some comparable institution: freemasonry or a political party, a social or political ideal. "Without the Church there is no salvation" becomes "Without the party there is no salvation" or "Without the community..." The secular cause takes over for the religious and furnishes, in turn, the same protection. Whether or not one is a believer, it is convenient to be able to get support from someone else, be it a counselor, prudent friend, individual, group, or institution. If that source of help in times of need also happens, by some strange circumstance, to be gifted with powers extending to the ability to change water into wine, multiply loaves of bread, heal the sick, and bring the dying back to life, what a resource! What a boon! Of course, there must first be a postulate, a belief in those powers. As it happens, the believer postulates them because he or she needs them. This leap from hope for a miracle to belief in its realization is readily comprehensible. So is the magic temptation to hasten its arrival by the repetition of certain practices.

Dependence

Messianism

In his heart, the dependent is waiting for a messiah: he hopes that the provider will inaugurate a messianic era in which all anxiety will disappear and every need will be met. Messianic attitudes are not peculiar to adherents of a religion. A messianic attitude is present every time a person expects a radical transformation of his existence as the result of an absolute event or as a result of the acts of a supernatural being — God or his delegate, "anointed by the Lord" — of a visionary, national or revolutionary leader, "guide," "father of the country," an entire group considered as a unit, party, sect, or movement, or just any person imbued with exaggerated worth, made into a savior, master, guru, or model. In the past, young girls expected marriage to completely transform their lives. Their Prince Charming must have had a strange kind of charm: "He was my God, my whole life," they would wistfully say later. The result is always the same: a new person in a new world.

That is why there are such violent reactions if anyone attacks this edifice, even verbally: the very equilibrium of the whole individual or collective personality is at stake. It is a defensive violence that becomes offensive through madness. It is the adherence of the members as much as or more than coercion that gives the key to an understanding of the influence and persistence of sects. The promise of a totally different life makes coercion tolerable; without that window on the future, the members would feel completely walled in. So, as paradoxical as it seems, the political or religious dependent who surrenders his life is actually saving it.

That is an extreme, reached most often in religion and politics. But every culture more or less assumes that role. Even children look to an imaginary world for refuge, protection, and compensation in the face of their weakness and fears. According to Bruno Bettelheim, fairy tales, whose origins are said to be ancient, are attempts to respond to the anxieties of young children and prepubertal adolescents. The kings and queens are the good parents, the sorcerers and wicked stepmothers the bad. Their adventures prefigure the difficulties of life and teach us how to surmount them. If the story has a happy ending, it gives the child hope for a happy resolution of his or her own problems. I remember how eagerly and tirelessly I used to listen to my mother, or our only household helper, tell me about the marvelous odysseys of the heroes of *A Thousand and One Nights* or the ruses of Jeha, the most popular character in the oral tradition of the Mediterranean area. Without completely believing these tales, I would become provisionally capable of crossing seas, bringing down ogres, and escaping from enemies; and, as a reward for my exploits, I would be given the hand of the sultan's daughter. At such times I was far away from the terrors of the dead-end street where I was born and the depressing atmosphere of my father's store.

Artists, it has often been noted, are somewhat like children. Regardless of the degree to which they may get carried away by their passion and be dependent on their art, they admit that there is an element of play involved. That is something the believer and the politician refuse to concede, out of fear that their influence might be diminished. Art is a fictional construct that knows it is such and for which that characteristic is, in fact, the justification. That in no way diminishes its richness and vitality. The activity of artists orders and serves as a catalyst for their whole psyche, bringing it to focus on works of art that are unique. That uniqueness and those peculiar riches, intuitively perceived by others, ensure the social legitimacy and material success of artists. Artists create models with which people can identify, in which the difficulties everyone experiences are recognized, described, and mastered in some way. That is the service the reader avidly expects from artists.

As long as men and women live, therefore, they look for help from the constructs of their own minds or from the contributions of certain more fertile individuals. The imagination is one remedy for anxiety, and certainly one of the most appropriate, because it is stimulated in accordance with the necessities of each particular anxiety: we invent or look for the story that is pertinent to whatever is bothering us at the moment.

Interpretations, diversions, and dreams, concrete tools, ways of life as well as fictions — culture is all of that. It is anything that allows us to solve the problems that arise from our contact with nature, with others, and with ourselves. And among these responses, the fictional provider isn't always the least efficacious.

The Uniqueness and Interchangeability of the Provider

The provider has two characteristics that are apparently mutually exclusive: *uniqueness* and *interchangeability.* In the depths of dependence, when the dependent is feeling deprived, she sees the provider as unique, irreplaceable because the provider alone can fulfill her expectations. If the dependent were to become really deprived, however, if she were absolutely convinced that she was going to be alone, she would immediately start looking for another provider and would eventually find one.

We all know how fiercely the peoples of the world defend their cultural values, which, they maintain, constitute their very being. In a sense, they are right. What would a durable group be without that spiritual community that is the foundation of its identity? And yet, when we examine a collective life over a period of time, we find new elements along with the stable ones. I have proposed to define culture as the aggregate, more or less coherent, of a group's responses to its conditions of existence. I would readily add that it is an aggregate subject to change: conditions evolve and continual adaptation is necessary for survival. To be more exact, it is an aggregate in which, in the long run, the new elements become dominant or equal the original ones. There are successive borrowings from neighbors, who are changeable themselves; from enemies, who have been victorious in battle or dominate by virtue of their economic and cultural ascendancy; or just from those among the vanquished who are more accomplished. The culture of a people is a harlequin suit in which the added patches are sometimes more extensive than the original cloth. But that doesn't affect its importance. For the people concerned, that suit is theirs, the only one they have, fashioned over time according to their needs and without which they would be naked and ill at ease. Nevertheless, there is hardly any such thing as a pure culture, and every culture changes surely and imperceptibly. The question of collective identity, whose importance we are finally starting to recognize, should not make us forget that identity is at once both constancy and transformation.

It is the same for individuals. An individual's feeling of identity is that of a continuity, but in the face of change. Nor are we any more unique for others. Everyone is familiar with the role an infant plays in the lives of a modern young couple. Everything revolves about the infant — the daily schedule, the organization of the couple's leisure, and even the arrangement of their house. Yet one child replaces another, and the newcomer receives all the attention of the parents, who often handle the situation so badly that the older child suffers. And when, one after the other, all the children have left, a dog will fill the bill almost as well. A child will consent to sleep alone if an animal or a toy takes the place of the parents. Anyone who is in love

would describe his own case by paraphrasing the words of
Montaigne: because she is she and I am I. To which popular
wisdom appropriately replies: "One lost, ten found" or "No
one is irreplaceable." Our experience gives us good reason to
think that both statements are true. The fanatic's fixation on
an object provided makes it impossible to contemplate its disappearance without anxiety — until the person transfers her
dependence to another object and is torn by the thought of being
separated from that. To use another colloquial expression, a
dependent is, at heart, flighty — a fickle individual who goes
from one enthusiasm to another.

The mechanism is largely independent of the real qualities
of the provider. From among all the strictly identical cars
manufactured on an assembly line, each driver claims to
recognize and defend *his* car. Among the innumerable houses
for workers, all the low-rent apartment buildings, constructed
according to standard models and, to the untrained eye, indis-
tinguishable from one another, each proprietor stakes out her
territory, into which she transposes all her personal myths along
with her furniture — until she moves to another neighborhood.
The key to the paradox is obviously time: *the provider is unique
at any given moment but interchangeable in the long run.* Yes, there are
many men, many women on the earth, but, for the moment,
he, she is the one I want! — until the wind shifts.

All or Nothing

Until the dependent's mood, or the conditions of his existence,
change, the property of uniqueness in the kingdom of dependence
establishes the reign of the law of all or nothing. Lamartine nos-
talgically wrote: "You lose one person and the whole world is
depopulated." Jean Giraudoux has wittily replied: "You lose
one person and the whole world is repopulated." Strangely, they

are both expressing the same idea. Without the one we love, the world is a desert, says the former; it is our love for just one person that deprives us of the rest of the universe, replies the latter. Passion annihilates everything that is not part of it. When I say that I have eyes only for him or for her I am also saying that I am blind to the charms of all other men or all other women. Dependence entails both plentitude and austerity — concentration on a single object that, alone, must suffice. It is in just such terms that mystics speak of their God, certain professional people of their vocation, and artists of their art. Writing is for me both a vocation and a recreation, a source of concern and a pleasure, an obsession and a remedy. That can sometimes be troublesome or even dangerous. It is hard to see how any provider could live up to such expectations. A provider's benevolence would have to be infinite to quench such a thirst; it would have to be perfect in intention and totally adequate.

In the absence of that double virtue, which is decidedly rare, every relationship between a dependent and a provider is problematical, every dependence is infected with doubt. The worries, suspicions, and difficulties inherent in such a relationship are aggravated by the dependent's search for absolute security — and the near certainty that she will never get it. Little children can't stand to see their mothers even use the telephone: they hold on to their mothers' legs, pull on the wires, sing, shout, and do any silly thing to get back the attention that has momentarily been distracted from them. A mother might, if she's lucky, be permitted to knit, because she can still watch the child; he can catch her eye again if he looks up from his toys. "It's impossible to correct any papers," says a female teacher, "unless I correct with one hand and hold on to the baby with the other. I've graded hundreds of papers with a child on my lap." And it isn't just children. One of my relatives would invariably call us, under the pretext of having some urgent message, every time her husband, a childhood friend of mine, came to visit. She would ask him how he was enjoying his visit with us; she was making up for the fact that she was separated, albeit temporarily, from him. Dogs, like children, become disturbed if they see their owners expressing their affection for each other; they get between them and try to make the couple into a trio. They are vaguely apprehensive of being excluded from the new unit; they fear that it will deprive them of their ration of affection.

Insistence on all or nothing also explains what might be called the fragility of romantic love. Once a man or woman discovers that his or her partner has been unfaithful, it's all over; the relationship is breached, if not shattered, regardless of the often sincere efforts of the guilty party and regardless of the victim's efforts to forget. Why does that irreversibility exist? Why can't the relationship be as it was before? It is because dependence demands certitude: if there isn't total security, then there is no security at all. Of course there never was complete security, but the partners lived as if there were. Doubt goes in both directions: when someone is in doubt, he or she assumes fidelity. But then there is proof: something has happened. And if one thing has happened, anything can have happened. It is similar to the way in which the smallest leak in the hull of a ship creates a feeling of insecurity among passengers who had previously felt quite secure. Some ships, it is true, are more seaworthy than others. A hull with no obvious leaks can prove to be more fragile than one that is all torn up — a tear can be repaired. But a dependent is so demanding that if he doesn't feel totally safe, then he's in serious danger. A military leader has to be infallible: he may have had a long series of victories, but if he should happen to lose a battle one day, even if he is eventually victorious, there will be doubts about his ability and his image will be blurred.

Because he was, one time, unable to avert a catastrophe, he is liable to fail again. Death and adversity never miss a single chance.

An Inharmonious Duet

No thing or person is ever totally and permanently safe. No military leader is infallible, no fortification impregnable, and no elected official perfectly intelligent and reliable. A friend, a lover, or a doctor might some day prove to be unworthy of the confidence that has been placed in him or her. Because the dependent knows that, and has a vague fear of it, she suffers from it before it actually happens. Her expectations may be illusions, but her suffering is real; imaginary fears can be just as tormenting as uncertain hopes. Suffering and apprehension are part of every expectation and color every relationship between a dependent and a provider.

If dependence affects the image of the provider, the image of the provider has an influence on what is expected of him. People don't merely hope for a gift; they assume that it will reflect the capacity of the giver. The more they respect him, the more exalted their idea of him, the more they will be disappointed if his gift does not correspond to their flattering portrayal. To a certain extent they will always be disappointed because their needs and expectations will always be greater than the provider's response.

If there is a response: the provider may not be disposed to respond favorably, or even to respond at all. A doctor, jesting only slightly, tells the story of the meals that, when he was very young, his boss used to provide during working hours. Twenty years after the fact, he still vehemently denounces this man's "unbelievable stinginess." And yet the meals were, according to his own description, more or less the usual laboratory fare.

Dependence

The problem is that, despite the passage of so many years and despite the fact that he is now just as respected as his former superior, he still has a very high opinion of him: a person of his stature ought to have provided sumptuous meals. It is quite common for those who are entertained by wealthier people to react with scandalized astonishment. They are annoyed by the simple life of their hosts, whom they suspect of being avaricious. "If I had what they have. . . !" But why should wealthy people make every meal a feast? Mightn't they have problems with their digestion? And even if they were austere, what is scandalous about that? The truth is that the scandal is in the mind of the dependent. She considers the wealthy person, who is more powerful than she, as a potential provider. But not only is the wealthy person not always a potential provider, he may refuse to be.

The dependent, preoccupied with herself, does not pay enough attention to the problems of the provider. And the more the dependent demands, the more likely it is that she will make the provider distrustful or impatient; a provider isn't necessarily, by nature, generous and altruistic. If, in addition, the provider shows any reservations, he confirms the suspicions of the dependent, who immediately becomes disillusioned. The provider's refusal to play the role assigned to him is proof of his treachery.

There is always a margin between what is asked and what is offered, between the hopes, which are unlimited, and the response, which is necessarily relative. In that always gaping trench desires proliferate, crazed by false expectations and wild figments of the imagination. That trench is also where the dependent's resentment and, often, the provider's guilt begin to develop. *The relationship between a dependent and a provider is a duet, but it is an inharmonious duet.*

48

The Dependent and the Provider

The Margin and Resentment

The gap between the demands of the dependent and the resistance of the provider can hardly be bridged because it isn't subject to the will of the partners. In each of us there exists, to varying degrees, a diffuse dependence that is continually searching for a provider. But no sooner do we get one than we begin to find fault with him because we want more than he could possibly provide. So anything is fair game and no one is good enough for this important and thankless role: parents, friends, public agencies responsible for social services, the government, or, vaguely, "they." We simultaneously beseech and condemn them all. We will always be dissatisfied with anyone from whom we expect so much and who fails to respond, or responds so poorly, to our wishes. We will always resent anyone who has any power that he or she could use to bestow a constant stream of benefits.

This supposes, moreover, that what is provided is, in essence, free. But that is true only in certain cases, when there is a gift. Ordinarily, everything has its price. Of course the connection between what is provided and the price that has to be paid is far from obvious. It is the result of a long apprenticeship. A child takes for a long time without giving anything; she slowly discovers the pleasure she can give or deny her parents. The adolescent makes the difficult, painful discovery that she will soon have to offer something in return for the subsistence, education, and leisure that have been provided for her. Experience and reason eventually convince the adult of the necessity for this exchange.

But no one ever completely accepts the idea. One of the causes of criminal behavior is the rebellion against this contract, which is perceived to be restrictive and excessive. The provider, whether an individual or a group, arouses ill will and suspicion. Would he, by any chance, be trying to get the maximum and give the minimum? That may well be what irritates us about "merchants" — they are people who have goods we covet. But they won't just let us have whatever we want; they make us pay, and even pay as much as they can get. "They're profiteers, starvers," we say, or, going a step further, "thieves." Some tradespeople, no doubt, may act like speculators, but that does not apply to them all.

It's about time, in the face of the current prejudice against business, for a renewed awareness of the social and historical role of commerce, which was a link between the nations of the ancient world and has been the unifying force of modern times. The fact remains that the tradesperson is a provider and, as such, arouses hostility. A poster plastered on certain walls says: "——— Stores — We're here to serve you." On one of these someone wrote: "And to make sure you pay!" The anonymous annotator was expressing indignation at what appeared to be a disgraceful fact. It's a fact, but not disgraceful: why shouldn't a business establishment, which performs a service, be paid for it? The answer is that, for a provider, gifts are supposed to be the rule, not the exception. However, since the truth is just the opposite, resentment against the provider appears to be inevitable.

Ambiguity

Nevertheless, the experience of being provided for is positive and the provider is a source of satisfaction. But that is exactly what creates the dilemma: the dependent expects so much from the provider that she is hostile toward him. The dependent's expectations are so high that she is bound to be disappointed, and the rest follows: disappointment leads to irritation, and irritation to malevolence, toward something that is, after all, to her benefit. When a baby is dissatisfied with his mother's breast, he bites it. This is nothing compared to what happens when he is weaned! In my native country it was the custom, once a child had reached a certain age, to put something with a bitter taste on the mother's breast, then laugh at the nursling's impotent rage. It was surprisingly violent for such a tiny body because this cruel joke aggravated the baby's frustration. The frightful barrier created by the bitter substance established an impassable frontier between the heaven of the past and the hell of the present. The breast, the source of so much pleasure, was suddenly inaccessible.

This same feeling of exclusion is part of our emotional response to the phenomenon of advertising. If advertising simply dispensed information, it would not be so irritating; but it proposes to provide things in a manner that is problematic. In the subway, the posters on the walls show us how we can satisfy our desires. Unfortunately, however, the train soon gets under way again, leaving behind it, in the dark, the splendors we have glimpsed. To make them come back would require sacrifices, money that we don't have or that it would be unreasonable to spend. In short, advertising proposes and consumers, while their imagination has been stimulated, can't always dispose. It's the old story of men and women struggling against the evils of temptation.

Dependence on a model illustrates especially well the ambiguity in every relationship involving a provider. The dependent wants to imitate the model because he admires her. But to imitate is, in the first place, to equal; then, as a result of the same impulse, to surpass; but to surpass is to dethrone. Not that the dependent ceases to admire the model or to be grateful to her. On the contrary, because he still has respect for the model, stands in awe of her, and is grateful to her, he has to keep trying. Gratitude, moreover, is not a completely pure emotion: to recognize what you owe others is also to acknowledge your own inadequacy. It takes a great deal of strength and pride, or placidity, to live with your own debts without worrying or becoming resentful. Ordinary mortals venerate their idols and expect them to fail. This seems contradictory, but it isn't: we are hostile toward anyone who helps us because we also have a need to defend ourselves against that person. I love this man for the good that he does for me, but I have to love him less in order to respect myself. That duality is accompanied by a self-perpetuating malaise. I begin by giving bad for good, which increases my discomfort. This new difficulty intensifies my hostility toward my provider, which adds to my guilt. The process of escalation is continuous. Conscious of the injustice I have committed, I admit, in advance, that I deserve to be punished for it, chastised by my benefactor, who is quite rightfully indignant at my conduct.

This brings about another stage. In the face of the supposed threat of my provider, I sense the growth within myself of a supplementary malevolence that, this time, is quasi-legitimate. The cycle goes on by itself. In spite of himself, the dependent more or less clearly manifests his embarrassment, which elicits some sort of negative reaction from his provider, which feeds the dependent's animosity and gives him the proof he needed against the provider. It all amounts to the provider's eventually being thought of as a creditor. It's true that anyone for whom something is provided incurs a debt that has to be paid someday and that such an obligation is unpleasant. The provider is even, to a certain extent, both a creditor and a debtor. She must give, because that is her function, and the dependent must, sometime, pay her back. In a way, the provider has a double advantage over the dependent. The word *must,* employed here in two different senses, is enlightening in that respect.

I have learned a great deal about this problem from discussions with my students, who are generally quite critical of their parents and teachers. They feel oppressed by them and bitterly accuse them of constantly trying to dominate them. Without directly contradicting them on that point — you can't deny what someone has experienced — I show them that the concept of oppression-subjection, which is otherwise so fruitful, does not completely explain their predicament. Regardless of what they say, they still have positive feelings toward their parents and teachers, an indication that they are not just victims of subjection. The students know that they will be supported, fed, and housed and that they will have money for tuition and recreation until they have finished their studies. This would not be the case if they were just dominated. They don't contest that; but they immediately retort that their parents are not disinterested. Their devotion itself is a maneuver to keep their children under control. They've brought them into the world in order to have someone to dominate. So, in a roundabout way, the students get back to oppression. Others, who don't go quite so far, suspect their parents of having conceived them in order to reassure themselves, so that part of them will live on after their death. They describe, sometimes with real traces of anguish, how their parents have projected on them their obsessions, their hopes, and even their idiosyncrasies. And there is some truth to that as well.

In this discussion, which begins again with each new brood, the younger generation is not entirely wrong. They are correct in denouncing, in the best of all the relationships in which a provider plays a part, the advantages enjoyed by the provider. Even in the case of love, something is received in exchange: the pleasure that comes from giving, the satisfaction of having an outlet or depository for existential anxiety, if not for the authority exercised on that occasion. But they are wrong to think that a valid relationship is one in which the provider receives nothing in return. Why, however devoted they may be, should parents, any more than the tradespeople mentioned earlier, be totally disinterested? What ethical or metaphysical principle says they have to be? When the question is asked directly, it becomes obvious that there isn't an answer.

What the younger generation is really looking for, more or less confusedly, is an absolute gift given strictly out of love. Since that is virtually impossible, they are disappointed, frustrated, and hostile. They are also frightened by the thought of the price they will eventually have to pay; they are scandalized and irritated by that inevitable part of the bargain. This kind of behavior shows that they are still adolescents; they won't become adults until they understand that there is no such thing as something for nothing because other people, even parents, also have needs, namely, the right to expect something in return.

This is true, of course, only in general. Among young people of diverse characters, some are already conscious of what their parents and teachers have, even relatively, given them; others will never become adults and will continue to make demands all their lives. Preoccupied for the moment with their own needs, young people hardly notice that others have needs as well. Their ability to notice is impaired by the fact that they imagine the others to be much stronger than they really are — so strong that they haven't any needs. I remember how, as a child, I was shocked, perhaps disgusted, to see my mother eating; a mother isn't supposed to eat, she's supposed to serve food to others. Parents should not want anything for themselves and they should not, in particular, profit from their power. But mothers do eat and fathers do find it satisfying to be fathers, even to the extent of enjoying their role as protectors. When it comes to power, the rule is that people seldom actually give anything away.

The Tendency for Dependence to Become Absolute

As I have pointed out, no one ever becomes completely adult. Which is why every provider should be prepared to respond to demands that are absolute. Every dependence naturally tends in that direction. A wedding ring is the first link in a chain. The lives of most married couples are such that neither partner ever has a chance to be alone; some of them have never, since their marriage, had dinner alone with another man or woman. Nor is there any question of either partner traveling or taking a vacation alone. Even the course of their thoughts should always be perfectly obvious: "What are you thinking about?" The question isn't necessarily a form of harassment, an expression of curiosity, or a way of being polite, but a reflection of vigilant anguish. If the other person isn't always there, even in thought, then you are alone. In one case in which dependence had already become neurotic, a married man could not be away from his wife for a night unless he had arranged for her to stay with friends. He finally got tired of that and left her. She committed suicide. He showed very little remorse. "I couldn't live," he explained. "Neither could she; it had to stop." He even seemed to be relieved and began to flourish again, as if he were rid of an anguish of his own, which in this instance would be that of the provider.

Mothers are well acquainted with this kind of anguish, the anguish of the provider. The constant demands, the uninterrupted pressure of their family, exhausts them more than the fatigue from their material tasks. "When I think about what I'm expected to do, I get frightened," a mother will often say. An only daughter, whose parents were very possessive, married a man whose parents had been deported by the Nazis and who, after years without a family, had a strong need for affection. They had a little boy who soon began to act like an only child by making excessive demands. "First I was an only daughter, then an only wife, and now I'm an only mother," the woman used to say with impatience that was half jocular and half bitter. One

Dependence

day she threw it all up and went off with another man. Contrary to the ideology of unconditional maternity and conjugality, women have less tolerance for the voracity of their children and husbands than is often thought: they simply obey ancestral commandments.

But traditions are not arbitrary. Women themselves find that they bring some compensation. The only daughter-wife-mother returned to her home a few months later. I can only conclude that she missed playing the role of absolute provider. This ideology corresponds to a reality: the need that avidly seeks its best object.

Literature, which contains treasures of wisdom along with a great deal of nonsense, has often presented us with a curious bit of nostalgia: the absolute object or, in other words, an absolute relationship between a provider and a dependent. Authors dream of a perfect work that would address every issue in a form ideal for the purpose. And readers hope for works that will respond to all their needs and give the greatest possible pleasure. Such a work would be what Balzac called ''the absolute masterpiece,'' *the book,* which would unite infinite wisdom and formal perfection, which would express, in sublime fashion, the soul of the artist and the soul of the world. That is what James Joyce was trying to do in *Ulysses:* Mallarmé, who was more erratic, never stopped talking about it. Many others did not talk about it but remained persuaded that they would someday write such a great work. Painters search for the secret that will allow them to penetrate to ''the essence of things,'' musicians for the composition that will reproduce ''the harmony of the celestial spheres.'' Even craftspeople never cease to hope that they can leave behind something lasting that will bear their trademark for eternity.

Is this folly? Is it a senseless hope or a game in which the players end up being more or less completely involved? It is one, in any case, at the the root of which is an active anxiety that maintains the creative fever. Writing or painting becomes the only way to relieve the tension. Every creative act is the union of a psychic outlet, a daily ritual, a source of pleasure, a contribution to society, and the promise of a work of art that is slowly taking shape. Such activity eventually comes to preoccupy artists body and soul; if they are deprived of it, they are devastated, unless, of course, their dependency relationship is somehow transformed. Consider certain writers who, without any apparent problem, just stopped writing: Racine after *Esther,* or perhaps Rimbaud. Other writers say to themselves: "As soon as I've finished what I have to do for the day, everything can come crashing down around me, I know that there is hope." Hope for what? Cold reason may ask the question, but we can surmise what the artist is suggesting: through my obstinacy, thanks to this continuous nibbling, I will leave my mark on the tree of time, I will conquer death and oblivion, I will save myself.

In religion we find the best example of an absolute interaction between a dependent and a provider. Here again we have the enlightening testimony of writers who have told about their conversion or their return to the faith of their childhood. Writers, unlike painters, are often very good at describing their own experiences. They are schooled in the art of introspection and have the talent it takes to put what they observe into words. By bringing together in connected fashion various remarks of Claudel, Cocteau, Max Jacob, and a few others, we can reconstruct a picture of the dependent-provider relationship pushed to its limit: the provider, in this case God, truly represents the absolute provider.

He seems to fulfill every aspect and every dimension of people's expectations. Let us see if that is indeed the case: *God is love,* that is, the believer has the feeling that he or she is loved. Furthermore: God loves more or less by definition, because it is his function; he offers his love in superabundance, just as the rubber tree yields its sap. God is such a source of love that he loves every member of the human race, even those who reject him. We can imagine the extraordinary tranquility produced by this perfect gift, which is not motivated just by the needs of the dependent but by an internal obligation on the part of the provider. An ordinary provider can change his mind, but not God. He couldn't do it — God or the natural and necessary provider. *God is pure love*; that is, nothing can tarnish it. God's love is made of fine metal and it is totally selfless. This does not stop the believer from offering little gifts and performing the ritual sacrifice in order to put herself in the good graces of her all-powerful provider, but those things are manifestations of the dependent's anxiety, not demands made by the provider. God does not expect anything in exchange; having no need of his creatures, he loves them without any afterthought or idea of personal profit. He is therefore completely above the kind of suspicion that inevitably falls on every other provider. He is moral and beautiful. This gives the believer, in addition to emotional certitude, ethical satisfaction and aesthetic pleasure (which are important to a writer). *God's love is, moreover, unlimited;* it can respond to any demand, no matter how avid. God can do so because his power knows no bounds, in time or in space. Last, *God is a person.* Coming after omnipotence and eternity, that appears to be restrictive; but it isn't: on the contrary, what the dependent needs most is love, in whatever form — approbation, esteem, admiration, passion. It is because of God that we have our relationships with those we love and who love us. God is the father-mother of each and every one of us; he is also the cement of every affection. Since God's love never fails anyone, we can be sure that we will never be alone.

Another writer, André Frossard, has told how he found God. He has also written letters to the devil, who, it seems to him, is not metaphorical. He has, at the same time, without attracting as much notice, told how and why he came to marry his wife: he experienced the same things and made the same discovery. Before he met his wife, he felt alone and ill at ease; the world looked gray. After he met her, he had the impression that he was, as he has said, finally talking to someone who was showing him some consideration. The end of his solitude brought him back to life, or to a more complete life; that is the way it looked to others, so that is the way it looked to him as well. At the same time, the world began to look much brighter, which we can take to mean that he could contemplate life again without being paralyzed by anguish. His experience with his wife, like his experience with God, was marked by the phenomenon of "rebirth" that I have described elsewhere in connection with political militants; militants speak of "sudden awareness," while those who are religious call it "illumination."

Once he or she has experienced this illumination, the religious person has a fixed point of reference that divides all time into two periods, the time before and the time after the decisive moment of conversion. In the time before, she was lost, abandoned, fragile, and endangered; in the time after, her eyes having been opened, she is no longer in danger, because now she knows and she can act. This is similar to the militant who has experienced a sudden awareness and has from that moment on a grasp of the truth about social relations and can act to change them. It is the whole personality, the whole identity, that is redis-covered and comforted by this new relationship with the divinity or the truth. It is the fruit of a love carried to the nth degree, human and superhuman, infinite and adapted to the needs of each particular individual. Let us add, in passing, that God not only provides for the individual directly, but also guarantees the order of the universe. In so doing, he protects the individual even more: order, calm, and security. To use the language of the social welfare agencies — and the coincidence is not fortuitous — God takes complete charge of us. He is insurance guaranteed against all unlimited risks.

While I was writing this book, it happened that I had to attend a funeral mass. That gave me the opportunity to see for myself how well the concept of a divine provider responds to the aggregate of human preoccupations. Religion is a system for providing what humans need that has been brought to perfection by centuries of development, and the Mass is a striking summary of all it has to offer. Everyone knows the frailties of the human condition: illness, pain, and death. Fear, guilt, and anguish are only varieties of pain. Human life is essentially characterized by three kinds of fragility: physical, moral, and existential. The Mass offers a justification for physical suffering and thus its alleviation, a pardon for our sins — that is, relief for psychic pain, and the pure and simple suppression of death.

The priest who offered the funeral mass was a decent sort, relatively simple, whose reliance on clichés only made him more typical. Through him, the Church was quite visible as the institution responsible for the organization of the ceremony and the custodian of the totality of its beliefs and values. The priest, the servant and authorized, "ordained," representative of the Organization, did his best to carry out the task that had been entrusted to him. And I think he succeeded: at the meal that followed the ceremony, which I also attended, the friends and relatives of the deceased had calmed down enough so that they were able to eat heartily and even make jokes. In the face of the stupor that results from bereavement, he had undeniably helped them to go on with their lives.

The Dependent and the Provider

He hadn't even tried to hide the practical utility of the whole affair. "If Christ didn't rise up from the dead, then what good is faith!" he exclaimed, echoing St. Paul. Jesus promised to abolish death. The proof of his good faith and of his power is that he was himself resurrected. He said, "I will come back," and he came back. What's more, he interceded for Lazarus and Lazarus came out of his tomb. At the least, there is hope for eternal life. So much for death. What will happen afterward? Good news: life in heaven won't be just a continuation of that on earth; it will be better. At the same time, as a result, life on earth is transformed because the fear of death is taken away and the future will be bright. There remains suffering, physical and moral. Think about it, says the priest: sickness and fear are nothing but preliminaries, antechambers of death. Once the fear of death is gone, there is no more despair. Suffering is no longer anything but a very brief interlude, a bad stretch on the road to eternal felicity. Life on earth is so insignificant compared to the other! It's Pascal's wager: compared to infinite eternity, the time we spend on earth is negligible.

You still have doubts? You're not sure you can, all by yourself, overcome your wretched difficulties, even by comparing them to the splendors that await you? Christ is still there. He takes charge of your hesitant weakness as well. He takes you by the hand; he walks ahead of you to confront danger and evil; he literally puts himself in your place; he receives the first blows. You still have a last glimmer of anxiety? Because your expectations are so great, you doubt that anyone can live up to them. It would take fantastic power, benevolence so intense that it would never be found wanting. Well, here is the crowning touch, the guarantee of guarantees, as Lloyd's of London warns all the other insurance companies in the world: Christ offers not only his sufferings, but his life in exchange for yours. He allows himself to be put on the cross, to be tortured, and to die. He takes upon himself in advance, on his own person, all the miseries of the world, just as a lightning rod takes the lightning. That is a marvelous, if not original, idea. Its lack of originality in no way diminishes its force; quite the contrary, because it works for so many people. The sacrifice of the Deity turns up frequently and under various forms: immolation, cremation, ingestion, crucifixion. Jesus allows himself to be both crucified and ingested. The ingestion of the host is an echo of the totemic feast but, the Church insists, "the real consumption of the body of Christ." The sacrifice and ritual consumption of their God allows Christians to partake of the immortality contained in that piece of flesh and that serving of wine.

The Death of the Provider

Christ promises everything, saves everything, guarantees everything because he makes the ultimate sacrifice: the provider can do everything because he gives everything. Or, to be more exact, he could do everything, if he wanted to — the myth of the pelican offering its bloody entrails to its starving offspring. The myth sometimes becomes reality, however, as in the case of the mother who throws herself in front of the car that is about to run over her child. It is a limitation, but that limitation controls the dynamism of the relationship between the dependent and the provider. Dependence tends to completely wear down the provider. Remember Père Goriot and his daughters. "I'd like to eat you right up," a lover naively tells his mistress, in the belief that he is showing her the depth of his passion. But what he means is "I would take all of you if I could," "You ought to belong entirely to me." Passionate love leads to the ingestion of the beloved. Is that really love? Does loving someone mean that you want what is good for him or that you want what is good for you? Anyone who really loves the object of his romantic passion would, it is true, want both — the demand and the gift, reciprocal and without reservations. The fact remains that such love is cannibalistic. And that is understandable. What better way to make absolutely sure that you won't lose someone than to transform that person, body and soul, into part of yourself? That's the method employed by children, the most primitive method of all — they put anything that interests them into their mouths. An absolute demand should be met with an absolute response, even if it means the death of the provider.

Of course it doesn't always happen that way. The provider isn't always sufficiently accommodating. Even if she were, she wouldn't always be able to provide what is expected of her. But that is what the dependent wants. He may not be convinced himself that the provider has the necessary power. He sometimes has the feeling that the provider is going to let him down; he has had the bitter experience of exposure to the provider's indifference, instability, and cruelty. But he has no choice: he so desperately needs what the provider can give! And if he's cornered, if his provider really does let him down, then he'll look for another one and make the same excessive demands on her. The demands will remain identical. And if nothing works any longer, if the evidence clearly indicates that there's no hope of getting help from any human source, he'll address himself to a source that is more powerful, more perfect, and capable of giving absolute guarantees. Here the intense attitude and the language of the revolutionary join with those of the religious person. "Revolution, in the depths of my misery I believe in only you" — this Revolutionary song has some of the accents of a psalm. God and the Revolution have the same function, whether they are constructs of the human mind or objective realities.

Dependence

Why Be a Provider?

In truth, there is something tragic about dependence. When one person is dependent on another, both the dependent and the provider live in the shadow of death. The dependent believes, rightly or wrongly, that negligence on the part of the provider would bring about her, the dependent's, destruction; and rather than perish she would kill the provider.

But why, if it's so much trouble, does anyone become a provider? That someone should make demands is understandable; that someone else should consent to respond to them is not so understandable. The provider lavishly dispenses whatever is asked of him: material or spiritual rewards, aid and affection — but all in vain. His work is never done, and he is never even sure that it is sincerely appreciated. Why does he tolerate insatiable demands? Why does he continue on a course that is fraught with so many difficulties?

The answer is simple. First, no one becomes a provider entirely of his own volition. He is more or less chosen for the role by the expectations of the dependent. The child or dog who watches you so intently while you eat has nominated you as her *potential provider*. You may decline the honor, but you can't stop her from imploring you with her eyes. The man or woman who gives you a certain kind of look, out on the street or at a party, has already indicated his or her desire for you. Such a person may, out of spite, even though you haven't done anything, become hostile, just because you haven't done what he or she expected of you. If a hitchhiker signals to you and you look the other way, he will sometimes insult you. If you refuse to give a tramp what he needs to buy a drink, he'll call you a cheapskate. This sort of thing can involve physical violence. Drug addicts who imperiously put out their hands for the ten dollars it takes to get

64

a fix will threaten to cut you up with a razor. Regardless of how you feel about what the other person wants, about hitchhiking, alcoholism, or drugs, you have been chosen as a potential provider and you're expected to transform yourself into an actual one.

This kind of personal pressure, followed at times by acts of violence, can be translated into a legal obligation. It is against the law to fail to give assistance to someone who is in danger; nor can anyone abandon a child or elderly parents with impunity. So, in certain cases at least, the law has recognized an individual's obligation to provide something to someone else and has pre-scribed penalties for anyone who fails to do so. Chances are that more legal obligations of this sort will be recognized in the future. Who would have thought, only twenty or thirty years ago, that the right to good health would be so universally accepted? That demands for job security would become commonplace?

But most of all, an individual becomes a provider because he or she has something to gain from it. No unilateral demand, or even any agreement, oral or written, personal or legal, will stand up very long unless both partners to it get something out of it. In other words, we have to assume that when someone becomes a provider, it is not just because she is constrained to do so; she always more or less consents to it. Giving pleasure is a way of getting pleasure. Our angry young people are right — anyone who brings children into the world and feeds, clothes, and protects them year after year does so because he or she gets something out of it, even if it is only the overwhelming emotion that grips every new father and mother. But they are wrong when they say that a provider should not enjoy that benefit.

As a precaution, however, let us distinguish between *parasitic dependence*, which is all to the advantage of the dependent, and *symbiotic dependence*, in which there is some advantage for the provider as well. No parasitic dependence is going to last very long. As a matter of fact, there is in almost every dependence, even if it is apparently parasitic, some sort of symbiotic relationship that is denied or camouflaged, out of shame or hypocrisy. Parents don't always care to admit that they get great satisfaction out of their parental role. They're afraid such an admission might make people think they are less devoted than they appear to be. But it's fairly easy to show that many people have a veritable *need* for children. It would make more sense to recognize what parents owe to their children and what children owe to their parents. We ought to admit that there is probably no such thing as a pure gift, that the most selfless gift is beneficial to the donor. It manifests his generosity and proves how powerful he is. The magnificence of the gift makes the donor magnificent. In the most extreme case, the absolute provider can be considered either as someone who provides absolutely for the dependent or as someone who absolutely dominates the dependent. He who can provide anything can do anything; he is master because of his strength and because of his generosity. It's a tempting role. La Rochefoucauld's analysis of human motives was acccurate, but he should not have sneered: human relationships are based on exchange, and it's better that way. Anyone who does not think so is looking at things through the childishly greedy eyes of the dependent.

We could at this point consider being a provider as a form of dependence. In his *Red Beard*, the great Japanese filmmaker Kurosawa shows how his principal characters, especially doctors, find their reasons for living in providing for others. Their devotion is only the visible aspect of a more complex interaction that gives them respect for themselves and peace of mind. It is reciprocity that explains the tenacity, continuity, and stability of the human duet. When lovers say, "I need you," they are doing more than just admitting that they're fragile. This statement reassures the other person by giving him or her a sense of importance. It also means: "The fact that I want you to be concerned about me guarantees that I will be concerned about you; you can count on me, because I need you." The implicit motto of those who are devoted to others is "I need people to need me." That isn't a cruel scheme. These people are respectable providers, doing something for themselves by doing what is best for others. And why not?

The only problem is that this double-edged complexity does not satisfy the dependent; it does very little to calm her fears. She was hoping the provider would be the solution to all her difficulties and she discovers that he isn't even completely devoted to her but is preoccupied just as much, and perhaps more, with himself. She was looking for a benefactor, and she finds a schemer. As her anxiety increases, she will demand more, in order to be better prepared. The provider, feeling the jaws of the vise closing in on him, takes fright and strives to keep his distance, if not to get further away. This humiliates the dependent and confirms her doubts. The cycle seems to be endless.

Can Dependence Ever Be Satisfactory?

The relationship between the provider and the dependent is positive, but can it ever be totally positive? It is unlikely. All we have to do is ask the question the other way: Is there any such thing as a dependence that is free from danger? To answer yes, we would have to assume the existence of a dependence in which satisfaction would be completely and definitively guaranteed. That is to say, a carefree dependence and a perfectly unstinting provider: heaven on earth. What usually happens is that the dependent always demands too much, and the provider never gives enough. The story of the pelican also

Dependence

illustrates how parents are horrified by the insatiable greed of their offspring. In my native country [Tunisia] my fellow citizens, with their natural exuberance, used to come right out and say it. ''You're eating my head!'' ''You're eating my liver!'' exasperated mothers would shout at their children, whom, just a few minutes before, they had been hugging. Parents want to give the maximum to their children and, at the same time, keep a little for themselves; otherwise, as they see it, they would be swallowed up. In one of his works, Henry Moore, the great sculptor, has depicted a mother gathering her children to her and, at the same time, pushing them away. It is easy to see from the way her progeny are behaving that if she didn't push them away, they would devour her. A provider has to defend herself from her dependent. If she does defend herself, however, she appears to be doing something scandalous, becomes the object of accusations and, before too long, violence. If she doesn't defend herself, she perishes in her role as provider; she might perish from a hunger for love, but a person has the right to refuse to be eaten at all.

This difficulty is probably insurmountable. In our hearts, we know we are caught in the dilemma, but we can't quite resign ourselves to it. That is why, once again, we fall back on some tutelary power: God, a messiah, a philosophical ideal, or a political cause. That is why we so often wish that things were different: ''I envy people who are religious,'' ''I really wish I could pray,'' ''I envy people who have given meaning to their lives.'' But we're not entirely unaware that revolutions often turn out badly and that God doesn't always respond. The relationship between provider and dependent is the domain of reciprocal distrust. We try our best, without having much hope, to explain these failures: chance, ill will on the part of certain people, some hidden plan of the divinity, or even a romantic twist.

"The more we love, the more we punish"; the next time, things will go better. Some people might prefer the simple anger of the Sicilians, who, in the absence of God, start to blaspheme and call the Blessed Virgin "Putana!" or that of the Bretons, who take the bust of a saint who hasn't kept his promises, that is, who hasn't been a good provider, and dump it in a bucket of water. A dependent can even have resentment toward God. But if he does, it means he still believes in the possibility and legitimacy of an unlimited relationship with a provider. It would be more reasonable to establish limits to what is demanded and to admit at last that there is no such thing as an absolute provider or a permanent relationship between a provider and a dependent.

II

The Dependent
and Dependence

Compulsion

Viewed from the standpoint of the dependent, the matter is clearer than it is from the provider's viewpoint: *a person is dependent because he is compelled to be.* He can't act any differently; at least that is what he claims. "It's in my blood," confides the enthusiast. "I'm a smoker" is an open admission of defeat. This is the way I'm made, take me as I am. What began as an event has become an integral part of one's personality.

There are, to be sure, those who deny it. They prefer not to give themselves that kind of image; dependence isn't always held in high repute. It seems to be the opposite of liberty, which is deemed to be one of the highest values, at least in our societies. Dignity demands that one affirm above all his independence. Anyone who accepts submission is considered to be contemptible, perhaps dangerous. His cowardice could lead to the enslavement of the whole group. The least that can be said is that dependence is the admission of a weakness, an incapacity to find in oneself the resources necessary for subsistence. The dependent does not know how to live on his own and needs someone to take care of him. He can hardly take care of himself; he needs company, complaisant company who will love him and pay attention to him. "I need someone to love me!"

The dependent is far from disinterested: if he has attachments to people, it is not for the people themselves but for what he can get out of them. This is hardly flattering for the provider, who feels as if she is being treated like an object and not valued for what she is. Priests, whose dependence is obvious, are reluctant to describe their commerce with God in such terms. They are afraid it would be seen as a diminution of their vocation. They readily agree that they would find it "impossible to live without God" — definitely the sign of an inner compulsion — but they refuse to recognize that, unless it is suggested to them that such a necessity, which is a source of great satisfaction, is neither degrading nor surprising. Some lovers are hesitant about the compulsive aspect of their passion. They find it more romantic to proclaim that their love is a pure impulsive movement toward the one they love and, in the same breath, speak of the agony they will endure if they are not loved in return.

This confusion is further sustained by the general condemnation applied to the object provided, which is often considered to be disgraceful or harmful. Alcohol can cause the drinker to neglect his family and professional obligations; the alcoholic costs the government more for health care than he contributes in taxes. A lover's passion becomes the focus of her energies and diverts them from the interests of society. That is why the Catholic Church, among others, forbids its priests to marry. Family life, even more than sexuality, would become the exclusive preoccupation of those who tend the human flock. In short, psychology, ethics, economics, and aesthetics seem to unite to condemn dependence.

That is the origin of the whole mechanism of shame that surrounds and regulates the consumption of the object provided: one either hides from it, conceals herself from the eyes of others, or one employs a ritual, a ceremony that signifies a permission sought from the group and granted by it. The dependent obtains the collective indulgence if she has shown that she is powerless and if she obeys certain rules. One doesn't eat, one doesn't kiss in public, unless she has observed certain formalities, respected a code. That allows the group to modulate the satisfaction of each member, to tolerate it and, at the same time, keep it within certain limits.

This is not particularly distasteful to the dependent herself, who does not wish to be completely at the mercy of her dependence — it could turn into a bottomless pit, where she could lose her footing. In a vague way, she cries out for some sort of keeper. Everyone is familiar with the agonies, the repeated and often sincere efforts of a smoker or drinker to detach herself from her object provided, her relapses, and sometimes her resigned abandon. Often the only way out is to ask someone else for help. We know that some gamblers will themselves ask that they be excluded from the casinos. That *taking charge* is the essence of the method employed by the organizations who help alcoholics, smokers, and, more recently, the obese. They quite correctly treat dependence as a deficiency of the will. For the will of the dependent they substitute, temporarily, the will of the group, which imposes its own norms of conduct, issues a reprimand for every lapse, and is not afraid to morally punish the offender, who is at once the object of both solicitude and disdain.

These same organizations know, however, that if the dependent does not sincerely want to struggle against her dependence, failure is inevitable. Any program of therapy requires the collaboration of the patient. It assumes that her will is not irremediably damaged. If the dependent perseveres in her slavery, it is because she more or less consents to it. She could throw off her chains, or at least lighten them considerably, if she really wanted to. In a sense, she deserves what she gets, which is why the help that one nevertheless obtains for her is hard on her.

Dependence is as much complaisance as deficiency; good will, or, rather, bad will, has as much part in it as the absence of will, at least in the beginning. We should always bear in mind that the burden of paying for it is often onerous. In short, *if dependence is a compulsion, it is a relatively accepted compulsion.*

Pleasure

It is understandable that people are reluctant to admit their dependence. It's one thing to be dependent, but to consent to

Dependence

it! Worse — to enjoy it! The courts are somewhat indulgent when it comes to human passions, as long as they think they are dealing with a misfortune of which the accused is a victim. It would be unwise to give passions the least bit of acceptance; there would be an air of perversity in the courtroom. Look at the way people used to snicker at women who complained that they had been raped. Wasn't it true that they actually rather enjoyed it?

It is obvious, however, that dependence is an expression of the individual's desire to fill a void in his life. The object provided may be harmful, but if it does what it is supposed to do, it will bring relief and euphoria. A relationship with a provider is a crutch that has two aspects: it is a sign of weakness, and it would be better if the dependent could do without it; but, for the moment, if the dependent's crutches were taken away he would fall down. So it's a good thing that they're there. As long as the object provided is there, dependence is tolerable. What's more, it is often a soft pillow. After all, if I'm thirsty, what could I want more than to find something to drink? That isn't all; sufficiency isn't all there is to a relationship with a provider. We have to go further. The truth is that there is, in addition, pleasure: *pleasure is definitely one of the aspects of almost every relationship with a provider.*

There is pleasure as much as compulsion: "I can't help it, but I also like it." The smoker smokes because she can't stop but also because it is a source of pleasure. The same is true of anyone who drinks alcohol or takes drugs, hard or otherwise. People are not sufficiently aware of the pleasurable aspect of dependence, which has perhaps prevented a proper appreciation of the tenacity of such forms of dependence. Of course the matter is always more complex, and the complexity increases with the passage of time. But pleasure and personal profit are almost always there, from the beginning and as long as the dependency continues. When I was a child I used to see people smoking *takrouri*, which I later learned was hashish, and drinking *boukha*, our very familiar and familial fig alcohol. I remember such occasions as pleasant interludes during which people would observe euphoric practitioners of those arts without making any judgments about them. There may have been a touch of condescension directed toward people who exercise very little restraint when it comes to following their inclinations. At the very most, there was a bit of disdain for the spectacle they were making of themselves, which wasn't always aesthetic and hardly very moral. But there was also a visible tract of envy for those who "know how to enjoy life." It is suggestive that, in the popular parlance, the word *kif* signifies both hashish and pleasure. "To make yourself a *kif*" is the equivalent of "to have a good time," a good time that involves a certain ritual, a preparation that is like part of a celebration and proceeds in accordance with established conventions. The aperitif ceremony observed by the French population in Algeria, with its good-humored solemnity, a bit symbolic, would be a charming illustration of the idea. None of this was in any way deemed to represent sin, decadence, or misfortune. What people did condemn were the excesses, their effect on a person's health and on the fate of that person's family. As far as misfortune is concerned, when it did occur — much later — people had forgotten what caused it.

Enough of paradise lost. There is scarcely any need to defend pleasure — it can defend itself quite well without any help at all — or to underestimate its price, that is, the dangers of dependence. A systematic panegyric of pleasure would be as ambiguous as its condemnation (although it would be worthwhile to draw up some inventories of it, and whoever did so would be a benefactor of humankind). But it's easy to see why pleasure has a bad press. (Has anyone ever noticed that for each pleasure there is a corresponding sin?) It is a part of the individual that eludes the group, which strives to completely control each of its members. Pleasure without social control risks running counter to society's goals. The sight of a drunkard "sleeping it off" is disconcerting and disturbing. "He's in a world of his own," we say — he's behaving in a way that annuls his connection to society. On the other hand, useful pleasure is approved, celebrated. Conjugal pleasure, which, it is true, has been christened a duty, is blessed by religions and legalized by secular institutions. The reason is that it strengthens the cohesion of social life; thanks to procreation, it extends the family unit and guarantees to the nation continued power, not to mention moral integrity. The pleasures described as "noble," those derived from the arts, music, painting, or literature, are praised because they are supposed to be different from ordinary enjoyments. The presentation of a sublime piece of oratory, the communication of elevated emotions, the revelation of a metaphysical universe are all much more than simple diversions. Moreover, the social interaction of which they are the occasion is a very important part of their prestige. An unknown poet is treated with disdain, while a poet who has gained recognition gets respect. The status of religious ecstasy, even though it touches on a domain where reverence is the rule, is, on the contrary, still ambiguous. It is honored as long as it appears to contribute to the fortification of religion; but it is suspected, and even combatted, if it ends up disturbing the institution of the clergy. Career satisfactions, honors, and the various rewards of success are generally approved because they are proof of group esteem. Except, of course, by those who are in opposition to the group, which actually reinforces the opinions of the group.

The ambiguity of pleasure, our hesitant attitude toward it, and its often real dangers should not make us forget its important and constant role in almost every human endeavor. Pleasure — or, to be more exact, pleasures, because there is a whole constellation of satisfactions — always plays a part in dependence. The ingestion of food is necessary for survival; but associated with eating is a specific enjoyment that comes from the taste of the various articles of food, which act on the taste buds, and from the stimulation of the mucous membranes. This latter pleasure can, in fact, be obtained directly, without any contact with food; that's why many people constantly put their fingers in their mouths. There's also the pleasure that comes from the euphoric prospect that one's stomach will soon be full, which is reassuring for the individual as well as the species. Kissing, in addition to being the occasion for that pleasant suction on the lips, gums, and tongue, serves as the herald of a more complete pleasure, which in this instance is erotic pleasure, the sign and promise of a reciprocal emotional exchange. Smoking is at once a compulsion, a "bad habit," and the accumulation of several satisfactions: suction and ingestion, but also manipulation and ritualization, which give the smoker a certain bearing, help him to conduct himself in society, facilitate communication, and make it easier to overcome anxiety. And these effects are not just the result of autosuggestion, a psychological crutch. Nicotine eventually acts as a narcotic, of course, but it does promote the synthesis of serotonin, a cerebral hormone that pleasantly titillates the nervous system. Laboratory rats injected with nicotine do seem to find their way out of labyrinths more easily. That obviously does not alter the fact that both tobacco and alcohol have undesirable effects. There is no doubt that smoke leaves residues in the pulmonary alveolae that cause them to shrivel up and lose their elasticity, resulting in increased risk of chronic bronchitis, cancer, and vascular disease. The cilia that line the walls of the respiratory organs are temporarily paralyzed and cease to function as filters. And it's hardly necessary to mention bad breath or yellowed teeth. The evils of alcohol are incontestable and have been known

Dependence

ever since people started to drink it, that is, at least since ancient times. In short, tobacco and alcohol are not innocent pleasures; but they are, it's equally obvious, pleasures.

If we forget pleasure, we will have seen only half the problem. We should, nevertheless, listen to the principal interested parties. Go back and read Omar Khayyám's poems about wine: he would rather drink a glass of wine than be caressed by a woman. He's not the only one: Baudelaire and Verlaine, to remain in the French tradition, glorified their alcoholic episodes. In addition to their guilt, when it exists, smokers and drinkers have a certain malice toward those who don't indulge. Such people, they say, don't know what they're missing; they're talking about something they haven't experienced — which is often true. There are, in particular, innumerable jokes and anecdotes told among drinkers, who like to represent themselves as "initiates," members of "confraternities" whose purpose is a certain pleasure known only to them. The expressions we use these days are not so hard on gamblers, drinkers, and smokers. "To get loaded" suggests behavior that, when all is said and done, is socially acceptable; the sight of someone smoking a pipe is rather reassuring. A middle-aged person who has a love affair is not judged too harshly and is sometimes even secretly envied. On the other hand, anyone who has "no vices" is suspected of some hidden sin. Anyone who has never been in love is looked upon with pity. It's unfortunately the same story in the case of the most dangerous drugs. If you listen carefully to a drug addict, you find to your consternation that along with compulsion, imprisonment by drugs, escalation, abandonments, and misery, there is the fascinated avowal, the fond memory of strange pleasures.

It is quite clear, then, that dependence is one of those amazing two-headed creatures composed of obligation and desire, necessity and satisfaction. This dual characteristic is specific to many forms of human and animal behavior, and perhaps vegetable behavior as well — after all, the plant that turns toward the light must be satisfied, because it does open up.

Need

What explains dependence itself? One remark before I start off in search of an answer to that question: While the temptation to look for an ultimate factor, a first cause or final end of all behavior, is inevitable, it is also true that no one who yields to that temptation will ever be totally satisfied. The temptation is inevitable because knowledge is like a staircase built in such a way that every landing offers a view of yet another one, to which one can't help wanting to ascend. No one will ever be totally satisfied because knowledge is also an endless spiral. Driven by curiosity, we never give up trying to find out what lies at either end. The wise thing would be to content ourselves with relative knowledge, because there probably are not any ends. Thought, at that point, becomes confused, and language becomes metaphorical. So why do we still try to go another step further? Because the next plateau does, after all, give us a better understanding of the previous one. I just hope that if I fail in attempting to explain dependence, it won't spoil for the reader the few modest results I have already achieved.

Having taken these precautions, we can ask the question again: what explains dependence? Or, to put it in a more convenient form, what purpose does it serve? What is its finality? Once the question is put that way, we can see that the answer is obvious: *dependence always attends a need.*

The two principal characteristics of dependence, compulsion and pleasure, are also aspects of need. We learn that from daily experience. As soon as there is a need, there is the potential for dependence. Even a cursory analysis confirms that wherever there is some need to be satisfied, there will be dependence. Conversely, wherever there is dependence, there will most likely be a need. A dependent individual or group is one involved with another individual or group in a relationship based on need, in which the latter furnishes the former with whatever is needed. That is the verdict of popular wisdom: to be in need is to have need of others. On the other hand, the pleasure associated with dependence comes from the satisfaction of a need.

This parallel analysis could be carried even further. A need that isn't satisfied creates a void that demands to be filled, with the help of others if the person can't do it alone. And what if the person fails and other people let her down? What if the void isn't filled right away? Then she'll become increasingly uneasy. And what if that uneasy feeling doesn't go away? Before long there will be anxiety and even panic, which can lead to a behavioral disorder. Throughout this description, the word *dependence* could almost replace the word *need*. An ordinary smoker of tobacco, not to mention a drug addict, may, if she is out of cigarettes, exhibit behavior that is surprising given her normal personality. "There are times," says one smoker, "when I feel as if I might do anything. I've even gone out on the street at ten o'clock at night, like a madwoman, to look for someplace to buy cigarettes." That is truly anguish, more or less acute, and the fear of being submerged by it. There is very little difference between this woman's behavior and that of a nymphomaniac or a woman on drugs, or who is "in a bad mood" if she hasn't had any coffee. While it isn't always as extreme, the behavior of a dependent, like that of a person in need, is oriented toward getting satisfaction as soon as possible.

The correlation with need makes it possible to answer a certain number of questions about dependence. For example, is there an unlimited number of ways in which a person can be dependent? The answer will vary according to whether we focus our attention on need or on that which makes it possible to satisfy it. If we bear in mind that needs themselves are not unlimited, then the answer is negative: the varieties of dependence are enumerable. What deceives us is that we are living at a time when desires come and go with great rapidity, especially in the wealthy countries of the world, which are deluged by the inventors of the industrial age and by the feverish productivity of our economic systems, which are constantly stimulating our appetites with new products. But if the objects of desire are infinitely variable, the fundamental needs and the dependencies that derive from them could be satisfied by just a few instruments of survival. In the midst of the most sophisticated toys, a child will revert to the same simple gestures appropriate to the manipulation of an old top or a doll. Among those who, in a multitude of different ways, stimulate our desires, the only ones who really touch us are the ones who bring back memories and make us feel some profound emotion.

That, it should be mentioned in passing, is the difference between a work of art and one whose appeal is based on the ephemeral surprise produced by its novelty. The impact of real art is felt in the depths of the psyche.

Desires and False Needs

We cannot, of course, adopt a way of life so austere that it would not be human. People are weavers of dreams and avid consumers of myths. They never cease to embroider upon and fantasize around their fundamental needs. Their field of vision includes the whole range of possibilities: bare wooden frames and finished buildings; solid earth and clouds; needs, desires, and false needs. In today's world, all those who are dependent in any way behave alike. They often act with the same intense determination regardless of whether the need they're trying to satisfy has its origins in a constitutional disposition — which can be either permanent or temporary; either present from birth, like hunger or thirst, or a later development, like the desire for coitus — or in a habit acquired under a particular set of circumstances, like the regular patronage of gambling casinos or racetracks. But there are probably correlations between these different kinds of behavior and our fundamental needs, and desires probably derive from needs.

There have been times in the past when, because of extensive damage to transmitters from heavy storms or sabotage, certain parts of France have been completely deprived of television. Those who were affected by such interruptions of service were very unhappy. Some of them claimed that they were often ill tempered and more irascible than usual; others confessed that they didn't know what to do with themselves at night, that they couldn't understand how they got through life before television came along. One young married woman said that life in her own home became so intolerable that she went back to live with her parents. She was clearly seeking refuge in the world of her childhood. Is this really a case of need? What does television do for us that makes the void it leaves almost impossible to fill with anything else? Since it hasn't been around that long, there is hardly any reason to suppose that people would be profoundly dependent on it. But the studies done among those who watch television have demonstrated that they are really lost without it. If we want to know why that is so — other than because there is a special kind of pleasure involved, which has yet to be analyzed — it would seem that we have to go back to historical precedents.

Let's suppose for a moment that the need for television is three needs in one: the need for knowledge, the need for communication, and the need for security. Knowledge is one of the keys to effectiveness; it increases our capacity to cope with the external world and even with our own bodies. Television, even more than newspapers or magazines, penetrates the solitude that envelops so many people, some of whom live in the middle of our larger cities; through its journalists and actors it provides a constant human presence that is not hostile but, on the contrary, benevolent. Radio has been providing the same service for years, and many people who live alone turn on their radio as soon as they get home, or even connect the switch on the radio to a light switch so that the lights and radio go on at the same time. That is their way of ensuring that they won't fall prey, even momentarily, to the anxiety they feel when they are all alone. Radio and television unite large numbers of listeners and viewers within a neighborhood, an area, or an entire country by presenting a single news or entertainment program that people can talk about with one another the following day, after having experienced it more or less together. Don't people sometimes call each other on the telephone if what they are watching becomes so moving that they must talk to someone about it? It's not outside the realm of possibility that we are witnessing the birth of a new relationship between the television viewer and the apparatus. There may eventually be a kind of video vertigo, or permanent visual shock — a morbid hunger for information that always leaves you wanting more, like the pungent sensation you get around your mouth, tongue, and palate when you eat something salty, or the irritating pleasure that makes us continue to consume sunflower seeds when we're no longer even hungry. Here again is a case of indulgence in a new activity to satisfy old needs. It has been said, quite aptly, that television is chewing gum for the eyes.

It's no secret that one of the minor subjects of disagreement between certain married people is reading in bed. One partner

Dependence

wants to put out the light and go to sleep as soon as his or her head hits the pillow, while the other wants to read a few pages, which bothers the first partner. The reader insists on having those few minutes. Why? For the pleasure? Out of curiosity about the end of a story? Just to be informed? Because it's hard to get to sleep? None of those reasons seems to be sufficient, especially in view of the fact that the other partner is often truly annoyed and hostile. Some determined readers agree that they read just for the sake of reading. "It really doesn't matter what I read — a newspaper, a detective story, or something more demanding"; "Sometimes I'm so tired that I don't understand what I'm reading, but I *must* read for a while."

Such a need obviously can't exist specifically for an activity like reading, a skill it takes years to learn. It would make more sense to assume that this desire, or false need, has replaced a necessity of earlier origin: reading in bed has probably come to be one of those rites of passage that mark the change from day to night and serve to combat the anguish we feel in the face of evening, darkness, and, perhaps, our rendezvous with the unconscious. "If I don't have my cup of tea, I won't be able to sleep." "If I don't pull the covers up over my shoulders. . ." Some married people can't get to sleep unless some part of their body is touching that of their partner. All this behavior is a response to the invincible, and very common, need for security.

In practice, of course, false needs and desires seem to be the very fabric of daily life. There is no doubt that pleasure is heightened by variety and surprise, which alleviate the monotony of habit. Since pleasure is such an important aspect of need, it is understandable that people get to the point where they pursue pleasure for its own sake, for the sake of novelty. But beyond novelty, the satisfaction of needs remains the ultimate goal. A Don Juan may float like a butterfly from one woman to another, but, when all is said and done, the outcome of the enterprise is always the same. So, in one way or another, *need is the key to dependence;* at the root of dependence you always find a need.

It might still be objected that all we have done is to trace the difficulty further back: to explain dependence, we resort to the concept of need. But what is need? If I say that need is the manifestation of the exigencies of life, that dependence is only one of the tools of that life, and that dependence is therefore just a particular case of a more general mechanism that includes it and accounts for it, we may have made a little progress, but why stop when we're going so well? I've already warned, however, that we have to stop somewhere or never stop at all. So I won't go any further in this regression. I won't resume the difficult, perhaps ill conceived, discussion of the nature of need. I'll content myself with a working definition: need is *a state of internal tension, innate or acquired, that demands a specific satisfaction,* even if it is in the form of a substitute.

We could take this definition in a broad or in a narrow sense. We could attempt to establish a classification and a hierarchy of needs, dividing them into fundamental needs and derived needs. We could try to classify the fundamental needs. We could either admit or deny that desire is nothing but need of which the individual has become conscious. But the definition is already sufficient to explain the relationship between dependence and need. If a resident of another planet were to come down to earth, the first time he saw someone inhaling smoke from little cylinders of dried leaves, lit at one end, and willingly remaining in that unhealthy atmosphere all day long, or saw still other people, who weren't thirsty, drinking strange liquids that sometimes made them lose their senses, he would find it incomprehensible — unless he had some intuition of the powerful physiological and psychological wellsprings of such behavior. That vital motive force is what I call need.

The connection between dependence and need is so close, in fact, that it has to be taken into consideration anytime anyone has occasion to deal with a manifestation of dependence. While dependence often involves quite individual behavior, its correlation with need will always be beneficial.

I have suggested elsewhere that the way to get a precise picture of a given dependent would be to ask three questions: *Who* is dependent? *On whom?* And *for what?* We can add a fourth: *to what need* does the dependence correspond? The answer to this last question will tell us something about the kind of satisfaction the dependent is looking for, about the sufficiency of the object provided, and, perhaps, about the nature of the provider. It will tell us something, in short, about the specificity of every case of dependence that commands our attention. In each case: why is this person dependent?

Dependence and Physiology

I have dwelt at length on the relationship between dependence and need so that I could also play the devil's advocate. When we come right down to it, how could dependence not have physiological roots? How could it be otherwise? We would have to have our heads way up in the clouds to think that there could be a psychological activity independent of the body. When a man looks at a woman, or a woman at a man, and it happens that one of them experiences a desire for the other, how can we distinguish the role played by physiology from that played by psychology? The point of departure here, as far as stimulation is concerned, is the sight of a potential sexual partner, which triggers changes in the body and in the mind. Conversely, any contact, even accidental, can generate mental images that are almost beyond the control of the will and physiological modifications as well. Whatever the point of departure might be, the cycle of events is the same. While it would be a gross and naive oversimplification to assert that the whole series of psychological events can be reduced to a series of physiological events, or that there is a strict parallelism between the two series — a theory that ignores the distinct character of each stage — the fact is that the correlations are close and quite apparent. The same can be said about anger, pity, or bitter memories.

The attention that is currently being paid to the consequences of toxicomania gives us the opportunity to increase our understanding of those correlations and that cycle. On the whole, dependence is an aspect of the dependent's physicochemical metabolism. Whatever the initial reason for taking a drug might be (anxiety, of individual or social origin; chance; the example of or instigation by a provider; the consequence of a previous dosage prescribed by a doctor), the result is the same: the establishment of a dependence. That is to say, a transformation of the dependent's metabolism, which transformation, from that point on, will impinge on his consciousness in the form of a painful psychological state; which he can dispel only by taking the same drug; which keeps his metabolism in its altered condition; and so on.

What if the dependent decides to stop taking the drug, refuses to satisfy the dependence it has created? He will find himself afflicted with both psychological and physiological disorders. To get relief from these disorders, he will be forced to resort to the specific substance that restores his equilibrium — until it wears off. Then he'll have to start all over.

It may soon be possible to give a more precise description of the process by which dependence establishes itself. We have only begun to identify the remarkable chemicals, known as *mediators*, that serve as relays between nerve cells, but this development already shows promise of being astonishingly fruitful. The union

Dependence

of the physicochemical sciences with computerized information processing will undoubtedly give us the key to many of the secrets of the extraordinary organ we call the brain. Computer experts are trying to arrive at an understanding of how it works, at least in part, and have even attempted to duplicate certain sections by artificial means. We now have some insight into what happens, physiologically, inside the brain and, specifically, into what happens when people take drugs like opium and its derivatives, particularly morphine. The brain is the center of the body's reaction to pain; it combats pain by independently secreting certain substances known as encephalins, which are similar to morphine and are powerful natural analgesics. If, for any reason, the future dependent has been given a first dose of morphine, that drug, taking the place of the encephalins, will settle in the brain.

But the visitor morphine is soon transformed into a cumbersome guest who, so to speak, perverts the host instead of helping him. Everything takes place as if the brain, having tried this convenience food, were beginning to like it. From that point on, the brain expects it, demands it as a regular part of its diet, so that it can do a better job of combatting the disorders it was previously able to handle with its own homemade concoctions, the encephalins. If it doesn't get it, it will show symptoms of a genuine deficiency, which result in episodes of pain for the individual. A dependence has been created that will require constant absorption of the foreign substance. Soon the body becomes habituated, or inured, to the substance and suffers the usual consequences — in particular, a diminution of the effects produced by the drug, a greater tolerance to it on the part of the nerve centers, so that it becomes necessary to increase the dosage to reestablish metabolic equilibrium. This is known as *escalation,* that is, increasing dependence and toxicity.

The close connection between physiological and psychological dependence is obvious. Someday we will be able to isolate in a test tube a "dependence enzyme," or perhaps several such enzymes, just as we can now demonstrate the relationship between adrenaline and anger, or between lactic acid and fatigue. Some researchers have already succeeded in making rats dependent on alcohol and they are trying to follow in the laboratory the genesis, evolution, and completion of their dependence.

Dependence and Ambiguity

The preceding discussion shows that the ambiguity of dependence is an aspect of physiology. Dependence means deficiencies and subjection, compulsion and malaise, with, at the end, the restriction of a person's liberty and inevitable toxicity. We might reasonably expect, therefore, that people would reject it, that they would be horrified by it and condemn it. The fact is, however, that they accept it and even go out of their way in search of it; and they excuse it. The key to this contradiction can be found, once again, in the consideration of need. Need, when it manifests itself, does so in the form of a disequilibrium which, if it is prolonged, eventually turns into distress. But if the need is satisfied, it gives the individual a sense of well-being and sometimes even euphoria. We can see that ambiguity increases as we get further away from our primary needs and become more concerned with satisfying our desires. *Dependence brings happiness and misery hand in hand.*

In that respect the word *toxicomania* is perhaps deceptive. Taken literally, it describes a kind of behavior that, even when restrained, would be at the very least surprising — a bizarre and insurmountable urge to consume toxic substances. A rather strange perversity, exercised against the self; a kind of masochism. The ambiguity of dependence has disappeared, and all that remains is the negative aspect. But while there may be

Dependence

cases in which a person seeks toxicity for its own sake, as a means of self-destruction, or out of bravado, it is generally looked upon as an evil that has to be endured to obtain something else that is considered to be a good. So we would do better to replace *toxicomania* with *dependence on drugs,* which preserves the double meaning common to all dependent behavior.

Moreover, according to current popular usage, the word *drug* does have two different meanings: there are good drugs and bad drugs, medicinal drugs, which are beneficial, and toxic drugs, which are harmful. And sometimes the same substance is considered both medicinal and toxic, and with good reason. A given substance can be good or bad depending on how it is used, the quantity absorbed, how effective it is against the malady it is expected to combat, and the subject's resistance. That is the principle on which homeopathy is founded and which, for all practical purposes, underlies every medical prescription. A pharmacist is a sort of drug dealer who sells his or her wares only to those who have a doctor's prescription. If a substance is beneficial, we call it a medicine; if it is harmful or if its effects are undetermined, we call it a drug or a poison. The difference is not in the objective nature of the substance but in the purpose it is expected to serve and in our mastery of its use as a treatment, that is, in its relationship to the dependent. Conversely, there are times when a drug acts like a medicine. If the word hadn't already been appropriated by the medical profession, the best general expression, one that takes in all the others, would be *remedy,* because in every case it is a question of finding a *remedy* for a painful condition, for physical or psychological suffering. This fact is reflected in our speech, in such locutions as ''home remedy'' and ''drastic remedy.'' Many people use alcohol for this purpose; and whoever thought up the clever idea of selling little pills filled with whiskey knew what he was doing.

The Dependent and Dependence

We may lament the fact that people feel the need to use substances that, depending on the individual's mood or the state of her metabolism and nervous system, stimulate her or calm her down, tranquilize her or make her euphoric. But there is no denying that people do need such substances and have for centuries in just about every part of the world. If someone were to draw a map of the world in which colors were used to designate the different areas where people drink alcoholic or fermented beverages, use tea or coffee, peyote or cocaine, chew kat or smoke various substances, there would be very few patches of white. People obviously don't deprive themselves, and never have deprived themselves, of the opportunity to get help from chemistry, whatever its stage of development might be. And why shouldn't they get it? Only a person who had no acquaintance with intense pain, in his own body or in that of someone close to him, would say that they shouldn't. Why, if he has the means to do so, shouldn't an individual fight whatever ails him, even if it is imaginary. For there is more than just physiological pain, traumatisms, or functional disorders; a psychic malaise can be just as intolerable as chronic bronchitis. There is more than just external aggression of the kind that is committed against human beings and that they commit themselves because, to survive, they have to struggle against nature, against animals, and against other humans. People also have to defend themselves against potential dangers; they have to dissipate fears that arise from dangerous eventualities that sometimes become realities. The various drugs that can be found in almost every civilization and every period of human history have undeniably helped the individual conquer anxiety in the face of permanent insecurity. In that respect, there is no *natural* difference between a minor stimulant, like coffee or tea, and the hardest drug. A doctor might just as well prescribe caffeine as morphine.

Dependence

The Price of Dependence

So does every difference disappear? Does everything happen for the best? Obviously not, for there is a price to pay. And that price is more or less high. The other side of drugs is their capacity for harm, and the degree to which they can harm someone is the measure of the price that has to be paid. In the final analysis, a dependent's behavior is determined by his or her assessment of the advantages and disadvantages of a particular object provided.

But there is always a price to pay. Every dependence costs something because every advantage has to be paid for in one way or another. A dependent expects help and favors from her provider; and she knows very well that she owes something in return, even if the idea does revolt her, even if she does try to get out of it and regardless of any dodges, alibis, or poses she might employ. Even an animal intuitively understands this. A sick or wounded animal can usually tell the difference between a new attack, which will add to its misery or finish it off, and something done out of pity, in an attempt to help it out. Dogs will endure, with amazing stoicism, the most painful forms of treatment, looking at you all the while with an expression that suggests gratitude as well as resignation. They'll lick the hand that tortures them for their own good because they sense that their pain is salutary. They accept the price they have to pay to get well.

These considerations may make it possible to clear up a misunderstanding. After World War II there was a great deal of controversy about the way some of those who had been deported had conducted themselves. There were allegations of real complicity between the victims and their oppressors. Having spent a little time in a work camp myself, I can say that, except in very rare cases, what took place was something quite different.

The Dependent and Dependence

I would prefer to call it resigned consent, a *connivance* imposed by those having the upper hand and more or less accepted by those subject to them. Complicity supposes voluntary collaboration between two parties for the purpose of inflicting damage on a third. When we consented, without putting up the least resistance, to perform some task that had been ordered by our guards, we were obviously not hoping for a Nazi victory but looking to gain time while we waited for the Reich to collapse. Only in that sense is it correct that the oppressor, in exchange for an insignificant concession, gets a certain amount of consent from the victim. This sort of arrangement is nothing new. The French historian Le Roy Ladurie has remarked that victims of the Inquisition cooperated more readily with an inquisitor from their own area, a fact that the authorities naturally put to use. Should we condemn those unfortunate individuals, who, in their desperation, were begging for the least glimmer of humanity? Does that mean that they blessed their dogmatic oppressors? When the Nazis made use of quislings, governors recruited from among the conquered population, they were not doing anything that had not been done before. And it didn't make the people hate their governors any less. On the contrary, the quislings were accused of treason and were assassinated more often than other occupation officials. But as long as the occupation continued, the quislings were needed to keep the population supplied with goods, to perform official functions, and to deal with the Nazis. Temporary submission is the price a conquered population consents to pay for its new state of dependence. That is what happened in the camps, not some willful complicity imagined by judges who must be considered unduly severe given that, at the time in question, they were spectators and were not exposed to the same dangers. It is true that, by extracting from their victims a relative degree of connivance, the Nazis, like all

Dependence

providers, profited from their position. But the victims got something as well: a reprieve, a scrap of bread in exchange for apparent apathy. "Please, Mr. Hangman, just a few more minutes!" In the camps, where there was such terrible deprivation, every drop of life counted and the main thing was to survive; people did not attach much importance to false airs or even to the horror of the tasks that were imposed on them and that they more or less accepted.

That is what the literary and cinematic works created since that time have tried to suggest, with the historical and psychological distance necessary for the slow gestation of art. The scandals that have grown up around them can be traced to the same misunderstanding as occurred at the time. In *The Night Porter,* director Liliana Cavani shows a woman deported during the war who resumes her affair with her former jailer, a Nazi who had severely abused her. At first she wants to get revenge on him, to make him subject to her will, just as he had made her subject to his. She relives the experience of enduring sex under duress. But a series of flashbacks reveals that the terrified passivity with which she reacted in the beginning gradually changed to a perverse connivance. As she reenacts this psychodrama, she reawakens in herself that same ambiguity. Before too long, instead of just punishing her former tormentor, she also willingly becomes his mistress again because she still wants the pleasure he had once given her. From that point on they are in league together. The film became the subject of bitter controversies. How could anyone make love with a member of the S.S.! If it were just some run-of-the-mill oppressor who committed an occasional act of violence it wouldn't be so bad, but a Nazi torturer! That's stretching things a bit too far. The truth is that the politico-historical setting somewhat obscured the message the director was trying to convey — but it also helped put it across. The horror of that sinister epic, which has left indelible scars in the flesh of humanity, masked the essence of the problem, which is more general — the price that sometimes has to be paid for the privilege of staying alive. But at the same time, the deliberate choice of that cataclysmic epoch allowed the director to suggest that there are no limits to that price: yes, if you have to, you make love with a Nazi.

It is no accident, moreover, that this film was made by a woman and that the principal character is female. These circumstances give the work added significance. Many women deal with their condition in life in the same way as the protagonist of the film. Because they are dominated by men, they have to give them something as a tribute. And since the one thing women have that is most appreciated by men is their femininity, they more or less willingly offer up what is expected of them. In the continuous tragicomedy played out between the sexes, women are often relatively acquiescent because they get something out of it. That acquiescence is not a trait that women are born with, but the result of circumstances. One day one of the men in my camp went to visit a German officer in his quarters and came back with something extremely scarce (I don't remember exactly what it was — perhaps a loaf of bread). The rest of us, who were envious, asked him how he had managed to get it. He shrugged his shoulders and said, ''I offered him my ass.'' The only reason there weren't more instances of men bargaining with their charms is that there wasn't much demand for them. When we get to the point where more women are in dominant roles, we will see if more men don't offer their bodies.

We find the same analysis in another work created by a woman, *The Story of O*, by Pauline Réage, which was also made into a film. It is amusing to note that the preface, written by a man, is full of the usual incomprehension. In an effort to explain

Dependence

the behavior of the heroine, Jean Paulhan tells the story of the black people in Barbados who allegedly massacred their former masters because they refused to keep the blacks as slaves. This suggests that slaves accept, and even prefer, slavery; in that respect they are like women, who supposedly take delight in their submission and even in the worst forms of treatment inflicted on them by men. It is clear that if the analogy between women and slaves has any value, it is not because they both find subjection a source of pleasure but because the objective conditions of their lives are comparable. What did the black people in Barbados want? To continue to be exploited? To be humiliated, beaten, and sometimes massacred? Obviously not. Assuming that the story is true, why, after having been given their independence, did they have resentment toward their former masters? We have the explanation right in front of us: in the wake of certain decolonizations, the citizens of the new independent nation, who are ill prepared to take charge of their own destiny, end up with a very tentative government and often split into opposing factions. Economic disorder and insecurity appear to be connected with the departure of the colonizers. This sometimes engenders a certain amount of nostalgia for the old regime, not, of course, for its injustices and brutalities, its police and army, but because, like it or not, subsistence and calm were more or less guaranteed.

We encounter again the distinction between subjection and dependence: the former slaves in Barbados, like the former colonial subjects, regretted the termination of their *dependence,* which brought them peace and whatever they needed to live, even if they had to pay for it with their *subjection.* The same is true for the heroine of *The Story of O* and for women in general. What the book says, rightly or wrongly, is that women are prepared to suffer humiliation and violence as the price for the sexual pleasure and tenderness they expect from men. Paulhan is overjoyed: so women admit that they want sex! What a surprise! A surprise to men, that is. Men denied the existence of sexual pleasure in women for so long that they eventually came to think that women did not have any desire for it, did not know what it was. What Pauline Réage set out to do was to remind us not only that women have sexual needs but that they, like men, are capable of going to great lengths to satisfy them. That isn't masochism, or perversity, but simple dependence.

One aspect of the film, something that no one seems to have noticed, confirms this interpretation: throughout the story, it is O who makes the demands, because she is in love. At the end, her partner falls in love with her. So what does she ask him to do then? To let her turn the tables and burn him on the arm with a lighted cigarette; and he does. Now the roles are reversed, the man is the dependent and it is his turn to pay with humiliation and pain. That, as we know, is something certain women dream about. In the midst of all the controversy that surrounded *The Night Porter*, people failed to notice that the heroine ultimately consents to die with her former torturer. And that, after all, is more serious than making love, even with an ex-Nazi. Liliana Cavani's message is the same as that of Pauline Réage: the price a person consents to pay for dependence can be unlimited.

Consent and Resentment

Dependence involves both consent and resentment; it is simultaneously accepted and refused. That is why the term *attachment*, which has been adopted by some psychologists, seemed inadequate to me. It does not bring out that fundamental ambiguity common to all forms of dependence. It is that ambivalence inside of us, of which each of us is intuitively aware, that makes it impossible for us to look at the mechanisms of

Dependence

dependence dispassionately. The viewers of *The Night Porter* or the readers of *The Story of O* were irritated because of their own confusion. They were not completely unsympathetic toward the heroines, who were oppressed or, at worst, deranged, that is, oppressed from within. But they went along with it! They acted on their own volition! That couldn't be. But that is one of the things Pauline Réage and Liliana Cavani were trying to tell us. And the same thing had already been suggested to us by the few women who dared to open their mouths — but we're still only beginning to really listen to women. Women are dominated by men not just sexually, but in every way — economically, politically, and culturally. Nevertheless, their subjection is only half the picture. The other half is the fact that they make demands, have expectations, hope for satisfaction, and are often rewarded with nothing but subordination, humiliation, and violence. The emphasis on the sexual aspect of women's subjection, like the emphasis on that aspect of their dependence, comes from their special relationship to men, which is highly erotic. And that makes these so-called revelations more scandalous, like everything that has anything to do with female sexuality — the private preserve of men. But it isn't a characteristic of the condition of women or a purely erotic affair.

Ambiguity in the dependent's behavior shows up in his relationships with his different providers, from the person who supplies him with consumer goods to his spiritual model. Need implies expectation; so as long as the need is not satisfied, there will be worry and doubt. And the longer the period of expectation, the more worry there will be and the higher the stakes will climb. The dependent finds that, despite himself, the price he is prepared to pay keeps getting higher and higher, in the same way that the price of a glass of water rises astronomically as you progress along the route into a desert. And the resentment toward the protential provider gets more intense. In an extreme case, if the person guarding a well were to refuse to give up any water, he would be killed. When someone is in need — is dependent on someone else — it means that, at the very least, he will be exposed to the other person's indifference. But he may also be subjected to the other person's rule, which can be quite severe. You can "lay down the law" to someone because you are stronger than he, but more simply because he needs you. And it is only natural that, as his need becomes stronger, more compelling and pressing, the potential dependent becomes more subject to the will of his provider — or believes he is subject to it. How, then, could a dependent possibly regard his providers with the innocence of a child — assuming that children are really as innocent as we think.

What makes a person's relationship with her physician, for example, so dramatic is that there is so much at stake. Regardless of whether the patient's illness is minor or major, we see the same anguish emerge: the possibility that the physician will fail and the hope that he or she will put an end to our misery. What is involved is nothing short of an effort on the part of the patient to fortify herself against the possibility of total destruction, death. That is why the patient pays excessive attention to the doctor's personal appearance, gestures, and statements, to the point that she becomes suspicious and uneasy and starts putting interpretations on such things. What exactly did the doctor say? What did he mean? The patient gets upset at the doctor for talking too much or for not talking enough. He makes his patients spend too much time in his waiting room, or he doesn't come fast enough when he's called. Is that a sign of culpable and dangerous distraction or of reassuring serenity? He is too greedy — a familiar point of contention between doctor and patient; today, however, thanks to the existence of health maintenance organizations, it doesn't cost a patient any more to see a doctor than it would to hire a plumber or an electrician. But the public's attitude toward doctors has always been rather vindictive, a fact that is reflected in the works of Molière and Beaumarchais. Doesn't everyone have a story about a bumbling, irresponsible, ignorant, or greedy doctor? Everyone could also, of course, probably go on to name another doctor whose knowledge and devotion are beyond compare and who has the complete confidence of patients.

What happens between doctor and patient is a striking illustration of the ambiguity that characterizes every relationship between a dependent and a provider. When someone quibbles about a doctor's bill, what he's really saying is: "How can the doctor put a price on something so important to me? How can she treat my anguish so lightly? And isn't she there to take care of me (at no charge), to eliminate my fears?" Such sentiments represent another form of the child's claim that he shouldn't have to pay for the things people do for him. This very ambiguous expectation inevitably contains the seeds of resentment, which is a first cousin of frustration and fear. Resentment sometimes turns into hate, and even murderous violence, if the patient has reason to think that his doubts about the doctor's competence have been confirmed, if he believes that he has been irremediably abandoned to his solitary suffering. Doctors have occasionally been assaulted, or even murdered, although such incidents usually involve psychiatrists. Today, efforts are being made to put limits on the authority of doctors by making medical knowledge relative and by institutionalizing, as much as possible, the treatment of illness. Anything that makes people more knowledgeable, strengthens their character, and gives them greater autonomy is progress. It is hard to see, nevertheless, how there could be any profound change in the relationship between doctor and patient, which is based on the knowledge and power of the doctor but also on the demands of the patient. The doctor is powerful because the patient is fragile; and it is quite possible that the majority of patients actually want the doctor to have complete authority. In any case, the kind of resentment a patient may feel toward his doctor is not the result of simple domination.

It is easy to see, moreover, that there are two kinds of resentment, which are often found together in a particular life situation: one arises from domination, the other from dependence. The first is a response to an act of aggression, which is what all domination ultimately is. The second represents disappointment, frustration, or the fear of frustration, humiliation due to weakness. There is a bit of all that in the behavior of adolescents: impatience in the face of the real economic, political, and emotional power that adults have over them, that they have to reckon with, and that they find revolting, but also confusion arising from the existence of several possible models and the search for identification, which is both desired and feared. "I don't want any part of this world you've created," "I don't want to be like my parents," "I don't want to do what everyone else is doing." They will have to, however; and it is hard to see how adolescents, unless they are exceptions, could possibly escape from the usual monotonous, preestablished way of life, which is both protective and oppressive. Sooner or later they will get married, have children, settle into jobs, fulfill their civic obligations, and generally end up paying homage, by virtue of what they do if not by what they say, to the gods of the hearth and to those of their parents, and they will sometimes openly admit it. "For the most part, my father was right," "I understand now that...," "In spite of everything, I'm still grateful to them." They will punctuate such admissions with an occasional sigh, as they continue, in spite of everything, to believe that some of their difficulties are the result of the negligence, errors, or malevolence of their parents. That duality, that constant ambiguity, is what gives dependency relationships their inexhaustible richness. Dependence, which is inevitably connected with need, which is a sign of both deprivation and satisfaction, and which engenders both gratitude and resentment, has, like Janus, two faces.

Terminating a Dependence: Real Terminations

There is no law that says a dependent can't decide that the price of dependence is too high and the connection too onerous. A person can make up her mind to bring a particular dependence to an end — to fight a habit, to quit smoking, to eat or drink less, to relinquish a favorite activity or break off with someone she loves because the person is too much trouble, to dissociate herself from an institution, to resign from an office, to give up the practice of a profession, to turn in her party membership card, to leave a church. The list of terminations is as inexhaustible as the list of ways in which a person can be dependent: the history of an individual, like that of humanity, is as much the record of his terminations as that of his dependencies. Terminating a dependence can be just as painful as the dependence itself; if anything, it is more painful. After all, except in extreme cases, an established dependence involves more satisfaction than worry, more happiness than misery. The termination of a dependence means disruption, the end of a familiar situation, the threat of the unknown, and, before long, the pain of deprivation.

A person's experience of termination, like everything else, starts early in life. It starts with the child, who very quickly gets a bitter dose of it: the inevitable toilet training, then the terrible paroxysm that consists of being weaned, which is followed by all the other kinds of deprivation. Being deprived of the breast is only the first link in a chain that extends from birth to death, that helps to mold a person's character and to determine the nature of his relationships with other people, and that has repercussions on those around him, both providers and others. Again and again, in various ways, it takes the child away from his mother and the mother away from the child. After the terrible disappointment associated with being weaned, suddenly there is the first day of school, with the frightened child crying in the schoolyard. The young mother, who smiles through her tears at this lilliputian display of emotion, comes home from the beginning of the first school day with a heavy heart. The separations that mark the course of our existence, whether they are permanent or temporary, important or inconsequential, thrust upon us or the result of our own initiative, and the trouble or melancholy they bring us are nothing but echoes of those first deprivations. What is a romantic disappointment if not a dramatic kind of separation? Haven't innumerable monuments of our culture — books, films, plays, musical compositions — had as their theme the anguish experienced by two people who, married in fact if not in law, are so attached to each other that a separation is sometimes fatal? We should be used to such stories about people madly in love and the catastrophes that befall them, but we still respond to them with the same emotion: we beg to hear, again and again, *Romeo and Juliet, Manon Lescaut, Camille, Tristram and Isolde* — in words, on film, in music. Each time we hear one of these tales we are brought together through our common experience of this extraordinary bond, which is a source of so much happiness and which becomes a source of so much misery as soon as anyone tries to break it. We immediately understand, and sympathize wholeheartedly, when we hear the universal lament: "He's gone!" "She's gone!" "I've been abandoned!" We have some intuition of how it feels to be the

105

victim of such a tragedy, even if we've never had the experience ourselves, at least in the form of personal devastation and abysmal solitude. A romantic disappointment may also be a blow to a person's pride, a wound to her ego, which jeopardizes her idea of herself, but it is even more certainly a sign of the despair that comes from the knowledge that it will henceforth be impossible to satisfy her need for the other person. For to be in love with someone is to have need of him or her.

Emergency medical technicians know how intense the panic induced by feelings of solitude can be; when someone is hurt in an automobile accident, they have to talk to the victim, tell him what is happening, to keep him alive. If the victim thinks he is alone, he will let himself die. Survivors of shipwrecks die more from despair than from exhaustion. People stranded on deserted islands are more likely to go mad or become savages than to construct anything. The solitude of night is not the most propitious circumstance for someone who is suicidal. If you turn your back on someone who is speaking to you, if you refuse to answer him and openly chat with someone else, he will often bitterly resent it and feel the need to get revenge. Such behavior is not just offensive; it simply opens up old wounds. Statements like ''Nothing is more exasperating to me than someone who won't listen'' and ''You never listen to me'' can sometimes be the prelude to drastic action. When one person attacks another, it is as much a response to humiliation as an attempt to reestablish communication or force the other person to pay attention. The fact that separation from other people has such a profound adverse effect on an individual is what led society to create the prison, which satisfies the public demand for strict punishment. While the discomfort, bad food, shame, and harassment that go with life in prison are, of course, just as difficult to bear, the essence of this kind of punishment is something else: it is the lack of freedom, that is, solitude and the termination of the usual dependencies. There have been times in the past when a person could, if he had money, buy all sorts of things at the prison canteen, get the respect of his jailers, and even have a servant. What has scarcely changed is imprisonment, that is, separation. Today attempts are being made to find some remedy for the misery of incarceration. Unless something is done to reduce the solitude and exclusion that are so much a part of life in prison, it will remain fundamentally the same. In that respect, newspapers, radio, television, and, especially, periodic visits and furloughs are of much more value to the inmates than the transformation of their menus or a new coat of paint on the corridors — which isn't to say that new meals and paint don't have their importance.

Children discover the efficacy of exclusion by instinct, or from very early experience. When they boycott someone, they may be imitating the adult practice of making a child sit in the corner of the classroom — and they do it just as cruelly as adults do. Lacking the means to put their peers in solitary confinement, in a cell, they invent psychic confinement: "I'm not speaking to you," "No one will ever speak to you again." The person who is being punished can circulate and go about her business. She isn't even deprived of her freedom — she's just alone. If she tries to talk to the other children, she won't get any response; she can shout and they will pretend they don't hear her, don't even see her. She has become transparent; she no longer exists because no one recognizes her existence.

Adults have not done any better. When they put someone in prison, they are isolating him by physical force. But they know that a person doesn't have to be confined to be isolated. Quite the contrary: there are many other ways to effect a punitive exclusion. All you have to do is erect an imaginary barricade around an individual or group. You refuse to engage in any dialogue, to establish any sort of relationship. You will hurt the individual or group as certainly as if you had attacked them. Ignoring a person can be just as effective as taking strenuous measures against her. You can drive a person to the point of despair by permanently refusing to communicate with him. The person who refuses to communicate severs the psychological ties that connect her to the other person; in so doing, she isolates the other person as effectively as she isolates herself. A refusal to communicate is a negation, an annihilation of the other person. A suspension of diplomatic relations is not just a symbolic gesture: it has serious political, economic, and cultural consequences. The misfortunes known as exile and emigration are forms of isolation by means of geographic distance. The exile is free to form, if he can, new attachments, but he has been forced to break off all the associations that constituted the living tissue of his existence. And since every individual is the product of a complicated network of relationships with other people, the destruction of those relationships can result in damage to his personality.

*

We're discovering today that the problem of retirement from work is not all that simple. As long as the idea of retirement with a pension seemed to be utopian, it was one of labor's important demands; now the fact is that such retirement is available to everyone. Everyone has a legitimate right to rest. Employees should be able to stop working at some point without falling into poverty. But this legitimate demand has proved to be a poisoned trap. Those who retire die prematurely. According to the insurance companies, 30 percent of retirees die within two years after they stop working; given the average life span for the entire population, they could have been expected to live for at least ten more years. The retirement they have looked forward to for so long proves to be a severely trying experience.

The Dependent and Dependence

Now that people dare to speak out and, thanks to the media, get a slightly better hearing, we're beginning to see, to our embarrassment, that this extraordinary victory is also a source of anguish. If we think about it, it isn't so surprising. When a person is retired, she feels as if she is being pushed aside; retirees die physically because they have been destroyed psychically. This aspect is implied by the word itself: to retire is to retreat from the world, or, even worse, to flee. There's nothing wrong with that, if the person comes back from her retreat refreshed and better equipped to continue the struggle. For elderly people the retreat is definitive, with nothing to look forward to but death. They might just as well die right away.

Just as retirement is not a simple matter of repose, unemployment is not a simple matter of salary. We used to think of unemployment primarily in terms of financial distress; but for the first time in the history of Western societies, it is possible to give people money for doing nothing. That should make them happy, but it doesn't. They still want to work for what they get. The right to work — which is a surprising expression when you think of the biblical curse "In the sweat of thy face shalt thou eat bread" — takes on another meaning. The unemployed are not just short of money; they also suffer from the lack of any opportunity to use their skills. It is that exclusion that makes unemployed people all over the world, from the young men in Third World villages to the *disoccupati* of Italy who hang around outside the walls of old palaces, in city squares, and by public fountains, look insouciant, detached, and painfully ironic about themselves and their society. The tendency for young people to get involved in crime is not just the effect of living in a turbulent age. It is a sign and a result of the fact that they are not integrated into society. Perhaps we have entered an era in which work will no longer be indispensable and in which machines are actually going to replace people instead of serving them. If that is the case, we will have to change our thinking. We will have to completely transform the relationship between work and leisure.

It's already true that leisure is no longer the most highly valued thing in the world — if it ever was. In fact, it has always been defined by work — as a brief period of inactivity between two tasks. If leisure time is increased, it will not be filled with relaxation — if it ever was. The leisure civilization will certainly not be one in which everybody just relaxes; people can't stand too much time away from their work. When they are working, they can't be busy all week long — continuously dependent — and then do nothing on Sunday. So they putter around, go fishing, hunt, play, or take part in sports; otherwise, they just "go around in circles." A popular song says that "children get bored on Sunday"; they aren't the only ones. In any case, leisure isn't relaxation any more than relaxation is idleness. It is rather a question, in both instances, of changing over from one activity to another. Travel agents know that the worst thing they can do is leave their clients with free time. If they do, the clients will get bored, frustrated, and disoriented; and before long they will become aggressive and demanding, without realizing what is causing them to be so irritable. They get troublesome, greedy, and gluttonous and demand more food, comforts, and attention than they would ordinarily receive. In short, they act like children, because they find it frightening to be in new surroundings, away from everything familiar to them. They are quite obviously suffering from vacationers' fright. The psychology of the traveler could be a field of study all by itself (how many people, arriving in a strange city, will be eager to make any sort of new contact?). It is easy to see why vacation clubs keep their guests on such busy schedules that they get exhausted and why they organize so many "activities," that is, continuous diversions, that they are sometimes accused of being useless or even silly. Better to be criticized for that than for the opposite.

People complain that certain vacation resorts are overcrowded. Why do they flock to them? The truth is that they are more afraid of solitude and inactivity than they are of overpopulation. They dread the boredom that can come from being on vacation just as they dread the boredom that overcomes them on Sundays, because everyone finds it difficult to endure a suspension of the daily routine.

Imaginary Terminations

Our ability to tolerate terminations and separations is so limited that it has been the subject of allegories and even a metaphysic of exile. Like everything else in life that fills the mind with fear, the sufferings of the exile have been the inspiration for numerous creative works, of which the poetry of Ovid remains the prototype. The theme of prison, of which Piranesi is one of the most fascinating exponents, has haunted the imagination of numerous artists. There are also theological and religious versions of separation as punishment.

Excommunication is simply a mystical separation. While it is only a symbolic form of punishment, it does have some effect on life here on earth. The excommunicated person's relations with his or her spouse, children, and other family members become so difficult that he or she is a most unhappy individual. Even a sovereign who is punished in this fashion, while he may still be able to command obedience politically, can no longer sleep with his wife or enjoy the company of his children. It is like being all alone in a glass booth.

Exile is the principal theme of the Cabala: the separation of the soul from God is the worst thing that can happen in the

111

Dependence

spiritual realm, just as the separation of a people from their land is the worst thing that can happen during life on earth. It is quite likely, given the particular history of the Jews, that the first theme is an echo of the second: the exile of the soul is a symbol for the exile of the race.

Alienation was a theological idea before it became a psycho-sociological concept. According to the theological version, every member of the human race is, by nature, alienated because everyone is separated from God. The biblical account of the fall of Adam and Eve for having eaten the forbidden fruit and their expulsion from the Garden of Eden — their permanent estrangement from God — has fostered the nostalgic dreams of a multitude of people. Similar themes can probably be found in most cultural traditions. Because separation is one of life's most painful ordeals people have diabolically used it against one another. First it is a fact, then it becomes a myth. It is particularly conspicuous in paroxysms, but it turns up everywhere.

Let us note that theologians and metaphysicians, like psychologists and sociologists, deplore the dangers and sufferings that go with separation. I have shown in my writings on domination that separation is one of the marks of oppression. Kept apart from others by his or her oppressor, the oppressed person is adversely affected in almost every respect, sometimes to the point of partial destruction.

*

Not so long ago, in the wake of the campaign against smoking, we began to see a certain kind of printed notice posted in various places. I saw one in a taxi that said: "Thank you for not smoking." I found the wording quite courteous, and I complimented the driver on it. "You say that," he pointed out to me, "because you probably don't smoke; people who smoke get really upset about it. As soon as they see the notice, some of them make

112

a big show of smoking anyway. I've had passengers tell me to stop right where I was so they could get out of the cab." I discussed this with a friend of mine who smokes quite heavily and found that she had the same reaction; I asked her why she felt so strongly about it. "He has no right to tell me I can't smoke," she replied, with sudden irritation. "Couldn't you get along without smoking for a few minutes?" "Yes," she admitted, "but the very thought that I couldn't do it if I wanted to is painful to me." I've heard of people who refuse to enter any public building, like a museum, where smoking is prohibited. In short, a threat is enough by itself to make people experience the kind of anguish that comes from the termination of a dependence.

On the doors of a certain large food store is a sign that says: "We love animals, but please don't bring them in the store." The employee who wrote that notice is a good psychologist. With just a few words, he or she made it clear that animals, in accordance with the food sanitation laws, could not be admitted and, at the same time, reassured their owners, for whom separation from their four-footed friends is definitely painful. The notice puts the same amount of emphasis on the management's love for animals as on their exclusion. The customers might have expressed their displeasure in aggressive fashion by refusing to shop at that store. So the author of the notice has let them know that their pets aren't being excluded from the store out of hostility, since the management loves animals as much as they do.

"If you do that, I won't love you anymore...I'll go away." Statements like that make children shudder and can almost send a shiver up the spine of many adults. Most people, when they hear the words "national defense," are inclined to think in terms of quasi-sacred and terrifying duties. Everyone is supposed to be ready to "shed his blood" for his country, and to die for it

113

Dependence

is "the highest honor." People will even sacrifice their children for their country, which is extraordinary when you consider how strongly people, like animals, are attached to their offspring. Unless an individual endows his native land or country (or his class, or humanity) with religious or mythical significance, what he is doing in such a case is losing his life and that of his offspring to defend that which sustains them. I don't want to be disrespectful, or to imply that patriotism isn't important, but I must say that people who are fanatical about national defense remind me of the monkey who got his hand caught in a jar because he didn't want to let go of a fistful of nuts that was too large to pass through the neck.

Romantic Jealousy, or the Fear of Loss

Jealousy, at least romantic jealousy, illustrates the fear of loss very well. Envy is a painful fear of seeing others monopolize all the sources of things with which a person might be provided — all the food, all the desirable members of the opposite sex, all the honors; in short, all the goods of the earth. It is an understandable emotion, even if unfounded. The behavior of the person who is romantically jealous seems laughable or absurd. If a love tragedy is a story of separation (Romeo will never see Juliet again) or of the impossibility of reunion (Tristram and Isolde know that they will never be together again), romantic jealousy is a matter of imaginary separation. The pain that the jealous person feels is quite real, however, and can drive him to take drastic action. That pain can even have a consequence that appears to be normal but that is nevertheless rather strange: the destruction of the object of the jealous person's love. The jealous person helps, through his own actions, to bring about a separation and even to destroy the one thing in the world he loves most. Even more bizarre, the person can destroy everything, the other person and himself as well — because a jealous person will sometimes take his own life after having killed the object of his love. The result is that such a person, out of fear of separation, creates a radical separation.

This sort of behavior has its logic, however; a false logic, to be sure, but it is well known that false logic is quite efficacious in the realm of the passions. The dependent destroys his provider out of fear of living without that particular person, which he doesn't think he is strong enough to do. He can also destroy himself because it is essentially the same thing: life will become intolerable for him in any case. At least he thinks it will; for he can only imagine what life alone would be like, since it has yet to become a reality. But all he does is anticipate the catastrophe that will destroy him. By eliminating the cause of his difficulty, he eliminates the difficulty itself; with no one left to fight, the battle will come to an end. In *Othello,* Shakespeare goes out of his way to make it perfectly clear that Desdemona has not been unfaithful to her husband and has no intention of leaving him, no matter how much pressure people put on her. The fact is that she hasn't done a thing. Other people have put that poisonous idea in Othello's head; but he could have found out if it was true before embarking on the cataclysmic course of killing his wife and playing into the hands of those who were trying to ruin him. But jealousy is not the pain that comes from an actual loss. It is the pain that comes from what might happen: jealousy, or the fear of loss. The fact that Othello could imagine his wife being unfaithful to him was enough to drive him out of his mind. To be dependent on someone, or something, is to believe that you can't live without that person or thing. It is, again, the tragic aspect of dependence, the dark side of its ambiguity.

This analysis of *Othello* naturally leaves a great deal to be said

Dependence

about that admirable work and its principal character. Jealousy is also a type of resentment. "No one can do that to me!" — a wound to the ego and an illustration of the law of all or nothing. *Othello* is also the story of a man who does not belong to the race of white Europeans and who is ridiculed because of his origins, which makes his humiliation even greater. The place of dependence in this scheme is obvious, however. It isn't the loss of Desdemona's love that drives Othello mad, but the possibility of that loss. It is an imaginary fear — the fear of seeing his dependency relationship with Desdemona, which provides him with love and social acceptance, destroyed. The stakes are too high; such a fate has to be avoided at any price. That is precisely what most jealous people do, but their behavior often appears to be astonishingly maladroit and contrary to their interests. The difference between Othello and Alceste, the principal character of *Le Misanthrope,* is only a matter of degree. Both try to rid themselves of the cause of their difficulties by separating themselves from their objects provided. They are just products of different eras. Alceste lives in a society subject to law and order, in which a romantic disappointment no longer authorizes a person to kill. Othello lives according to a more primitive code of behavior; he smothers Desdemona under a pillow. Alceste decides that he will never set eyes on Célimène again; fortunately, it was possible during the reign of Louis XIV, if things were going badly, for a woman to enter a convent and for a man to go off to war. But the idea is always for the dependent to put some distance between himself and his object provided. To stop the terrible doubt that is eroding his relationship with his provider, the dependent destroys the relationship itself. And if it is impossible to destroy the relationship, he destroys himself. The result is the same: an end to his torture. The aggression that he wanted to direct against the cause of his suffering is directed against the dependent himself. Some people, if they are angry and cannot take it out on the person who's provoking them, will slap themselves or bang their heads against the wall. Others smash dishes or furniture or set fire to their house, the symbol of the home they both adore and detest. It is another way of using the energy that comes from suffering, by turning it in a different direction.

Retrospective Fear, or Romantic Disappointment

Where does such savage energy come from? It is definitely not generated by anything real, but by something imagined. A mother will slap her child when he shows up after being lost for an hour. Instead of being glad that nothing has happened to the child, she hits him, that is, she acts as if she were going to destroy him. This time it is not the fear of losing something, but the fear of having lost it. The energy from the mother's anguish was used up in her aggression against the cause of that anguish, even though the cause was a person she loved very much. Disappointed love is allied to this retrospective fear. People who are in love and who discover, to their disappointment, that the one they love has never been the kind of person they imagined him or her to be, are equally capable of committing murder or suicide. Anna Karenina threw herself under the wheels of a train. Her reputation had been ruined; but not every woman who finds herself in those circumstances commits suicide. She killed herself mainly because she had discovered the disparity between perfect love, which she believed she had found and for which she had abandoned everything — her husband, her child, and her friends — and the reality of her flesh-and-blood lover, whose idea of love was different from hers. She couldn't cope with the difference between her dependence and her object provided. Anna continued to be passionately attached to her lover, but she realized that she was just lavishing her affection on a shadow. From that moment on, her passion had no object and could never be satisfied. Her chosen solution was to destroy the relationship. But since she couldn't kill her lover, couldn't have any effect on a phantom, she killed herself.

Such behavior is not confined to novels. Defendants in criminal cases will sometimes, perhaps without realizing what is happening to them, give the court a bizarre explanation for their actions: "I loved her too much, so I killed her." They are telling the truth, however, because that's the way they feel. "I loved her so much that she never would have been able to respond to my need for her." Former priests or militants sometimes act the same way: "They burn what they once worshipped," others say; and they're right. But why do such people react so strongly? The strength of their disappointment is proportional to the strength of the expectations they had previously entertained. It's another version of what I have called, in connection with the mechanisms of revolt, "the return of the pendulum."

Scandal, or the Fear of the Void

Jealousy is the confusion created by the threat of a separation — a panic that leads a person to bash in her skull in advance or to bash in someone else's skull. It doesn't make sense, of course, but people can't always act sensibly. "Since I can't have this woman, or this man, no one will." Is this spite? Not exclusively; if my object provided continues to exist, even after my death, my dependence continues. The danger persists after death. The dependent can't tolerate even the idea of this after-math, so she suppresses all consideration of time. Everything has to be destroyed, both the provider and the dependent herself. Is this still just the stuff of novels? The answer is obvious, and it's time we acknowledged that there are such things as imaginary terminations and that they're just as disturbing as real ones.

In the same way, a scandal is a disruption created by a threat to the normal order of things — by a possible, or actual, termination of an established order. But any termination of an established order is painful, and it's easy to see that there are as many scandals as there are established orders: there are biological and theological orders, as well as cultural orders and the various social orders. People are scandalized by the sight of an elderly man kissing a young girl, just as they are by disease, physical deformity, or blasphemy. It is also easy to see that there are as many established orders as there are social groups and systems of values. What seems scandalous to some people is not scandalous to others. But it is always a question of defending some kind of stability that is being threatened — a rampart without which people would feel vulnerable. In short, when people react to a scandal, they are defending themselves as much as they are defending anything else; they defend a system of values to defend themselves.

A few years ago, a misguided young man made a bet that he could cook two eggs over the flame on the Tomb of the Unknown Soldier in Paris. He was arrested and sent to jail by the government. A quick survey of opinion on the matter reveals that, while some people thought the incident was funny, others, more numerous, approved of the punishment. A few apparently thought the man should have been handed over to a firing squad. The feeling was that one does not make fun of patriotism, any more than one makes fun of religion. For many people, the emotional shock produced by an ironic challenge like that is unbearable. The young iconoclast had not, however, destroyed anything tangible, any part of the national patrimony — that sort of offense could have been measured in terms of money and expiated by the payment of some kind of fine. But that is precisely the point: if someone burns a building or defaces public property, he can make amends. The man in question here had done something infinitely worse: he had desecrated a national shrine. To burn a flag, or to allow the enemy to take it away, is much more serious than to abandon a piece of territory. Such misdeeds strike at the very essence of the nation, which is not relative.

The norms and values by which nations live are supposed to be more or less permanent. That is why people have a tendency to look for counterparts of their values in some immutable order. The laws of nature on earth are, accordingly, said to be nothing but reproductions of those that govern the heavenly bodies, which guarantee them with the seal of eternity. Rights are divine, or "natural," which comes down to the same thing; and duties are "sacred" — even toward secular institutions. But again, there is no need to look for conceptual coherence. The myth is sufficiently revealing. The tablets that Moses used to promulgate the laws of morality to his people were copies that he had hewn out of stone after his famous fit of anger over the golden calf, during which he had broken the original tablets given to him by God. This is a point on which the Jewish tradition exhibits a kind of modest hesitation: we're not sure that the law we have is the original, but what we do have is an exact copy of the original, which is eternal. Regardless of whether they are mystical or intuitive, buttressed by philosophical arguments or held to be self-evident, values should be unshakable, no matter what happens. They have to be, so that people can cling to them the way they would cling, in a storm, to the mainmast of a ship. Women who serve as hostesses have known this for a long time. If you want your party to be a success, that is, if you want everyone to go home happy, make sure no one brings up any controversial subject. "No religion or politics" is a very wise policy, and one that English clubs apparently adhere to as well. Some people, who are otherwise quite civilized, can't help getting furious if anyone criticizes their church or political party. The singer Yves Montand, in an interview, poked a little fun at himself by telling how he and his wife, Simone Signoret, used to leave the table if anyone seated with them attacked the Communist party, to which they didn't even belong. They literally could not tolerate that kind of talk. I have seen people who have had such discussions remain completely estranged from each other long after their opinions on the subject had changed.

This is why religious people are so often irritated by nonbelievers (and why the reverse, for that matter, is also true, if the nonbelievers are dogmatic about it). Religious people, who have a firm grip on the truth and who live in felicity, ought to pity others for their blindness and insecurity. But they are often on guard, easily disturbed, and aggressive as soon as anyone says anything unfavorable about their beliefs. Why? They are shocked, they explain, by the lack of respect for religious values. But why is disrespect shocking? Because such behavior endangers what people *ought* to respect? Why should that which people ought to respect be respected? Does it need signs of deference from the very people whose opinion should hardly matter at all? How could such lofty values, such certain beliefs, or a superhuman being more powerful than anyone could imagine be affected by disrespect on the part of such negligible people? It always surprises me to hear people say that "the faith is in danger." How could the faith be in danger if it rests on intangible values? The expression "the death of God," which was invented by a modern thinker and which is so scandalous to religious people, seems comical, rather than scandalous, to me. If God exists, he couldn't die; and if he doesn't exist, he couldn't die either. How can we help but think that that isn't the problem? What's really in danger isn't religion, but the religious person himself or herself. Religion is that which binds a person to his God and to the community of the faithful. To attack it is to disturb those ties. It is easy to see how a religious person might find such a course of action scandalous — that is, dangerous.

In any case, religious people act as if they were overcome with anguish if anyone says anything negative about their system of values, and I understand better now why they react so violently. I have to admit that I have not always understood. When I was a young writer, I very imprudently criticized certain institutions that have been built up over the course of centuries to help people cope with life. Is it any wonder that people reacted with resentment, hostility, and even violence? I naively thought it was my "duty" to proclaim "the truth." But people had to be willing to listen to it. And why, for that matter, was I so obstinate myself in wanting to do my "duty"? One of my readers, who was a critic and writer himself, confessed to me one day that I had made him cry because I had written that the religious tradition could be used by certain people as an excuse. I thought his reaction was definitely excessive, if not bizarre. I understand it better now. If the religious tradition were nothing but an excuse (which, I should add, is not what I think), it would no longer have any value in itself. I was taking away his crutch. His emotional reaction and the hostility he felt toward me, which diminished with the passage of time, were inevitable.

I still remember the response, quite extraordinary for a philosopher, that the existentialist Gabriel Marcel once gave to a media survey of public opinion. The subject of the inquiry was an incident similar to that involving the iconoclast at the Tomb of the Unknown Soldier, in which a young bookseller, a Catholic in revolt against orthodoxy and the institution of the clergy, wanted to do something to get the Church out of its doldrums. He conceived of provoking a scandal right inside the Notre Dame cathedral in Paris, and he did just that. After it happened, members of the media interviewed various people about it. Gabriel Marcel said, in substance: "If I could get my hands on him I'd smash his head on the steps of the cathedral." That's just the sort of behavior you would expect from a vigilant and implacable defender of the temple that represents the values of the faithful, the sort of behavior that distinguished the great disciples of the faith, who didn't hesitate to burn heretics at the stake or to cut off their heads. The evil had to be torn out by the roots, so that the cause of the scandal would disappear, so that order, equilibrium, and security could be reestablished. And the philosopher in question had to fall apart as soon as someone struck a blow at the religion upon which he was dependent.

But there are other than religious and political scandals. Actually, there is no such thing as a scandal per se. Anything that threatens to disrupt a dependency relationship is felt by the dependent to be scandalous. There are dietary scandals and cultural scandals, fashion scandals and metaphysical scandals. Anyone who doesn't eat the same things we eat becomes the object of our curiosity, our amazement, and often our ironic or aggressive reprobation. We naturally think we have good reasons for condemning such a person, but when our reasons are examined in the light of reason they don't stand up at all. "Those Hindus! There they are starving to death and not only do they refuse to eat cows, they let them roam around on the streets!" But do we eat the cats and dogs who swarm all over us, right in our own apartments or as alley cats or stray dogs? "Well, we're not starving to death," people will retort. That's true, but the question remains: why do we eat rabbits rather than cats? Isn't it because we refuse to allow ourselves to eat cats, while we do allow ourselves to eat rabbits? In spite of all the jokes about

Dependence

putting the cat in the stew, we would hardly sympathize with an unemployed or utterly destitute person who actually cooked a cat or dog. And is it really the fate of the Hindus that bothers us so much? When did we start taking such a strong interest in the welfare of others? The real cause of our anxiety is something else: the attitude of the Hindus with respect to cows probably makes us wonder about ourselves. We will eat cows; they adamantly refuse to do so. There is something surprising and disquieting about that. We have the same distrust of people whose dietary habits are too different from ours. How can anyone refuse pork or oysters? You have to be weird or stupid! Why, however, do we eat rabbits and not rats, which look so much like them? "Rats are disgusting." Of course, but for a Muslim or a Jew, pigs who wallow in mud are just as repugnant as rats. At least those are the reasons they give for their disgust; here again, the matter is more complex. While the French love to eat frogs' legs, people from neighboring countries that are part of the same cultural tradition wouldn't eat them for anything in the world. I understand this very well because I feel the same way about snails, although I'll gladly eat pork sausages and tripe! The truth is that there is nothing more relative than disgust, and it is not a matter of cows, pigs, or rats per se but of our relationship with them insofar as they are objects provided. The same man who is so fastidious in matters of hygiene will tenderly kiss his dog on the same muzzle that the dog has stuck into all the animal excretions in the neighborhood. That merely amuses us because we would do it ourselves. But a person who finds "good, healthy milk" repulsive and who prefers to gobble up grasshoppers totally upsets our dietary order. Such a person seems to be condemning milk and forcing us to eat grasshoppers. What he is doing at the very most is depriving us symbolically — but who knows, perhaps someday he will do it for real —

of what seems preferable to us. He is suggesting to us that we should eat anything at all or die of starvation. That is why we get upset, are revolted, and fight back. By our irony or our anger, we put pressure on such a person to do as we do.

The same insecurity, and the same demands, can be found at the heart of any scandal over clothing. It is imperative to *us* that other people should wear the kind of clothing we wear. To make sure that they do, we resort, if necessary, to relatively strict rules that are sometimes codified and put into writing. Of course, everything that people do has more than one meaning. There are various reasons why a group of people might all wear the same type of clothing. They might do so because it is customary in their occupation: priests wear cassocks, and members of the military, athletes, postal workers, and police officers wear uniforms. They might do so for economic reasons: it's cheaper if a whole population, such as in China, wears clothing made from the same material and in the same style. Or they might do so for traditional reasons, which is the case with regional costumes. But the fact is that, when people expect everyone to dress alike, there is always some other reason as well. Children, for example, will persecute any member of their group who wears anything different from what they are wearing. I have a scar on my forehead that I got because of a silly hat given to me by one of my uncles. Anyone who dresses differently is already an unknown quantity and could therefore be dangerous, so we have to warn him or her by baring our teeth or by openly showing our disdain, which is another way of bringing down an adversary. We feel more comfortable, moreover, when we are dressed like everyone else, which is probably an atavistic reaction. Don't stray from the flock, or you'll become the target for any enemy who might come along. There is a certain pleasure associated with being different, which comes from self-affirmation, from claiming superiority rather than admitting fragility. It is hardly a question, however, of absolute originality: even this pleasure is codified and defined, explicitly or implicitly, with reference to the norms of a more restricted group existing within the society of which it is a part.

The fear of scandal is essentially the fear of disorder, and disorder is a threat to a dependency relationship. Most of the rules of practical wisdom that have been offered by the various ethical systems are guidelines designed to keep people from voluntarily or involuntarily interfering with other people's dependency relationships. The Ten Commandments, in addition to being principles of religion, are lists of things we should avoid doing if we don't want to create some type of scandal, that is, if we don't want to upset other people. Don't steal, don't lie, don't trespass on your neighbor's property — these are also bits of practical advice. Christ, who the Apostles said had not come to change the law, made such bits of advice into more than that. Just looking at someone else's spouse in a certain way is enough to make a person guilty of adultery. That was good psychology; both the person who is doing the looking and the person whose spouse he or she covets could be in danger. There are many men and women who can't tolerate the way other people look at their partners or the way their partners look at attractive people who pass by. In certain circles, looking at someone in such a way can be enough to start trouble. What happens, then, if someone actually does something? If someone trespasses on something belonging to you — your house, field, or car?

It is clear, in conclusion, that the more a scandal disrupts a dependency relationship, the more intolerable it is. Historians, even those who disapprove of the excesses committed by the Commune of 1871, are still amazed at the murderous fury displayed by those who were loyal to Versailles. Their reaction was proportional to their fear of losing their privileges. The hatred of those who advocate the common ownership of property, which has,under various names, been present throughout history, is shared by everyone who owns anything, regardless of whether his holdings are large or ridiculously small. It comes from one of the most common and most persistent sources of anxiety. The idea of a trespass against private property is related to the well-known tendency among animals to defend the territory in which they hunt and take refuge and to the tendency among people to defend their belongings, which are an extension of the self and a reserve indispensable for survival. Gold and silver and the various securities are an expression of power but also symbolic extensions of property. Middle-class families know that it is better not to get involved in business with relatives because it can interfere with relationships that are too precious in other respects.

Survival Devices

How can a person avoid the pain that comes from imaginary or actual separation? The pain that comes from disruptions of a dependency relationship, which are inevitable in any social situation? The answer is obvious. The person either fortifies the dependency relationship or fortifies herself against it; or she could do both. In any case, everyone has to learn to manage both dependence and its termination; life is a matter of constantly navigating between these two poles.

What is more universally positive than the practice of holding hands? In Western societies, only lovers and children are supposed to hold hands; in the Eastern Mediterranean countries young people of the same sex often do so in public. This simple gesture has a number of different meanings. There is, to be sure, the reciprocal tactile pleasure that comes from contact with the flesh of another person. But it also signifies: "Look, I'm not

carrying a weapon, I have no hostile intentions, I'm a friend."
And especially: "I'm here, I have no intention of leaving; I
couldn't even if I wanted to, because you wouldn't let me." A
multiplicity of ties is expressed in a single act. A slap on the back,
a prolonged handshake, or a hug would accomplish the same
thing. The image of an adult and a child huddled together, hand
in hand, in a hostile world, even in the middle of a desert,
suggests something reassuring: solitude has been vanquished.
Charlie Chaplin understood that and often made use of it.

In the culture of every nation the rites of integration and the
rites of passage sometimes coincide. Marriage ceremonies help
the individual to leave his or her own clan and to become a member of a new clan. Tom Thumb, to avoid getting lost, marked
his path with little white pebbles. We spend our lives doing the
same thing, leaving here and there little pebbles, either real or
symbolic, that help us to get back on the right path. That is why
every nation has its emblems and every age its insignia. Badges,
regional costumes, and uniforms encourage recognition and
solidarity. And what confusion, what unhappiness, at times,
befalls those who can no longer find their way! The current
concern about problems of identity is attributable, in part, to
the possibility that such a fate might become reality. "Our"
country, "our" native land, and "our" civilization are the sum
total of our points of reference — the familiar people and places,
the common language, the cultural traditions, the social rhythms,
and the dietary habits that reassure us and make life easier for
us. We soon grow tired of speaking a foreign language or looking
at new surroundings because we have to make a constant effort
to adapt. And we likewise vigorously defend our country — our
material, psychological, and spiritual comfort — and our culture
— the system of values and ways of behaving developed by successive generations as a solution to the problem of surviving in

the face of nature, animals, human beings, and even unknown dangers.

Because there's so much at stake, our tendency to behave this way generates a certain amount of friction. We expect our fellow citizens to do the same; if they don't, we treat them as if they were unpatriotic or even traitors. In other words, we accuse them of putting us seriously in danger, materially and emotionally. We've created the cult of the family, an institution that has gradually emerged from life in society to become the individual's protection against threats from without and within and that sometimes protects him or her from the excessive demands of society itself. We allow people to be massacred for the sake of religion, which is, it's true, one of the important parts of a nation's culture. We fight wars to "save civilization." Generally speaking, nations and individuals fiercely defend what they call their reasons for living and what it would be more exact to describe as their survival devices. I trust that no one will object if I decline to dwell any further on these phenomena, which I have elsewhere [in *Portrait of a Jew* and *Liberation of a Jew*] called *safety values* and *defense mechanisms* and which, together, make up the *survival devices* of a group.

Fanaticism

Fanaticism is nothing but an extreme form of self-defense, which often turns into a preventive attack. When someone mentions fanaticism, we usually think of the religious variety, but religious fanaticism is still just a type of cultural fanaticism. Just as there are several different kinds of scandals, which are related to the various objects provided, there are different kinds of fanaticism. When I was an adolescent I played amid the ruins of Carthage and, later, when I fell in love for the first time, my lover and I used to take walks there. Among the secular stones

Dependence

of the Roman theater, which basked in the gentle light of a sky that was always blue, there was a marble plaque commemorating the heroic martyrdom of two young Christian women, St. Felicity and St. Perpetua, who, rather than deny their faith, chose to be thrown to the lions. At the time, we hardly noticed it; when I think back on it today, their behavior seems very strange indeed. It isn't natural, after all, to sacrifice your life for the sake of convictions, religious or otherwise. It goes against the instinct for self-preservation, which is one of the most powerful instincts of all. How could anyone want to do such a thing? To answer this question by making comparisons with other kinds of behavior that can only be described as suicidal adds nothing to our understanding of the problem. And statements like ''It's always been that way'' and ''People have always sacrificed themselves for important causes'' are nothing but admissions of our inability to furnish an explanation.

While it would be presumptuous to claim that dependence can completely explain this type of behavior, there is no denying that it makes it much more comprehensible. The passion for truth, which excludes everything else and lasts as long as life itself, is probably a symptom of a more profound and more primitive emotion: fear. Truth is a rampart that has to be defended at any price because if that protection is lost, some sort of monster will appear and swallow everything. This sort of temerity would be more understandable among troops about to go into combat: the consequences of a defeat under such circumstances would be terrible, unforeseeable.

All of this, as the official ideology of the group, is naturally internalized by individuals and becomes part of their conscience, their soul, their system of values. If this is not the case, why do intellectuals, members of the clergy, priests, and scholars — those who specialize in things of the mind — fight so bitterly among themselves? Why do they take simple disagreements about methodology so seriously? Because they believe that they are defending the truth and that the others are mired in error? Because they love truth? Undoubtedly. But what does it mean to love truth? What is most surprising about those who love truth is not that they love it but that, like those who love rabbit meat or oysters, they worry that others don't. There is nothing wrong with loving truth; but why do people want to impose it on others? And why is it so much more important to them that anything else — so important that they will consent to sacrifice the lives of others and even their own lives for its sake? Isn't it because, without it, they would somehow feel as if they were in danger? I sometimes wonder if even Spinoza's *Ethics* might not ultimately be the product of its author's emotions. People often point with satisfied assurance to the adage attributed to Aristotle: "Plato is dear to me, but truth is even dearer." This is not only debatable, but hardly consistent with what people living today actually do. The average person will simply defend those who are close to him without bothering to find out if they are wrong, although he might, if he has a passion for justice, reproach them for what they've done. People spontaneously defend their way of life and the interests of their group: people before ideas. When Camus said, "My mother is more important to me than justice," for which he was roundly condemned by all the intellectuals in Paris, he was expressing this common attitude.

The insistence in ethics on the universality of the moral law and on the protection of outsiders and those who are weak is instructive — but *a contrario*. That isn't what people are instinctively inclined to do, and the truth is that it takes an effort. That is why people who do act that way seem fascinating and, at the same time, a bit less than human. Everyone knows about Thomas More, whose fate has inspired numerous writings. As lord chancellor of England, he refused to give King Henry VIII his approval for a divorce that was prohibited by the laws in force at the time. The king, after having tried to win him over, turned to threats, but in vain; nothing could make More change his mind; he preferred to die on the scaffold rather than give in. He left behind him the image of a hero with examplary fortitude.

But, above and beyond strength of character, what does this extraordinary rigidity signify? Thomas More was no doubt defending a conception of society that was different from that of Henry VIII: a social order in which law, and not the will of the king, is the ultimate authority. It was a conception that would, in the future, give the citizens of the realm more guarantees, freeing them from subjection to the will of a single man. His stand on this issue has made Thomas More seem to be a precursor of modern democracy. He paid for that with his life: he is a hero. What is a hero? It is a person who is willing to sacrifice himself or risk his own life. For a just cause, it should be added. Although that point is not entirely clear, because someone can be a hero for one group and not for another, and what seems just to one group won't necessarily seem just to another. But is it so natural to be a hero? We are so accustomed to certain ideas that we take them for granted. Isn't it surprising that someone should consent to die on the scaffold for the sake of an idea? Not if we assume that such a hero is constrained by some other force and that More could hardly have done otherwise. He was defending an image of himself, without which he felt life would be intolerable. That does not in any way make what he did less meritorious because, by his actions, he performed a great service for his community. But what he did was definitely ethical fanaticism, which is very much like religious fanaticism. If More had been able to, he might have killed the king; being unable to do so (it would, later on, be considered permissible), he allowed himself to be put to death. This is another instance in which someone took his aggressions out on himself instead of on the person who was guilty of disturbing the established order. Next to the lives of other people, the most important thing to him, more important than his own life, was respect for a system of values that gave meaning to that life. That still seems illogical: to save what gives meaning to life, you sacrifice life itself. But it isn't illogical when viewed from the perspective of dependence. Without that which gives meaning to life, the individual feels as if he or she can't go on living.

It is not so surprising, therefore, that people should quarrel, and sometimes even come to blows, over a piece written for the theater. That is just what happened at the Battle of *Hernani*,* in which young romanticists in red vests planted bludgeons on the bald heads of their older adversaries, who were themselves armed with canes. Conflicts between generations get resolved in various ways. But above and beyond such customary conflicts, and Victor Hugo's play, which aesthetically was only ordinary, each of the combatants in the theater that day was defending his own idea of the way things ought to be. The conservatives were defending an order to which they were accustomed and which allowed them to live in relative comfort. The young revolutionaries were defending a vision that would have allowed them to overthrow the established order, under which they were effectively excluded from any meaningful participation in society, and to create a new one under which they would have a better chance of realizing their dreams. When all

---

Hernani, written by Victor Hugo, was the first dramatic work produced by the Romantic school in France. When it was presented to the public for the first time, in Paris in 1830, traditionalists in the audience — those, that is, who favored the conventionally wrought plays of writers like Racine and Corneille — tried to drive it off the stage, and a famous riot ensued.

the picturesque details are disregarded, what it comes down to is that each participant in the Battle of *Hernani* was inspired by a different view of the world. For many people today, art has taken the place of religion because tradition has failed to provide answers to the new problems they have to face. As a consequence, and as a result of democratization, there has been a substantial increase in the number of people who take an interest in the arts. Such people talk of painting, music, or poetry with solemnity and are quick to take offense at anyone who doesn't; they treat works of art like sacred, priceless objects; they organize exhibitions that are like masses and they react with righteous indignation against anything remotely resembling disrespect. This sort of behavior comes very close to being artistic fanaticism.

Anything that aggravates a termination, separation, or abandonment, anything that disrupts a dependency relationship, is considered to be dangerous and immoral. Infidelity is unanimously condemned because it endangers romantic dependencies. On the other hand, anything that helps to bring people together, to establish or consolidate a dependency relationship, is considered good, legitimate, and desirable. Fidelity is unanimously praised because it is the sign of a firmly established dependency relationship.

Consequently, we are expected to go to any length to protect and strengthen our dependency relationships, whether they are real or ideal. This is the origin of the demand for absolute security. Sayings like ''Only the beginning is difficult'' and ''He that will steal a pin will steal a pound'' contain a psychological truth — that of an absolute beginning after which anything becomes possible, that is, the worst. ''One glass is too much,'' say reformed alcoholics; for, afterward, ''a thousand glasses aren't enough!'' We can never have too many moats, parapets, and walls. An expression Jewish people use is enlightening in this respect. They talk about "barriers around the law" and even of "barriers around the barriers"; and it is true that their survival as a distinct group is attributable to the persistence of their law. A hero is still someone who fights for our collective dependency relationships. His reward for that is universal gratitude — glory — and that internalized glory we call "the satisfaction that comes from doing your duty."

An individual or group will continue to protect dependency relationships even if they interfere with other people's dependency relationships. When I was in a labor camp I saw men fight each other, without any qualms at all, for a bowl of soup, a cigarette, or a place to sit — not just men without education, but men of all sorts, from every kind of background. This double thrust is an aspect of the most diverse types of behavior, types that seem to be opposites: racism or xenophobia, and dependencies that are considered to be noble. The new artistic schools* are not content with making new kinds of films or writing new kinds of novels; they claim that films and novels created by other people are out of date: the others have to die for them to live. And if someone else creates something so original, so obviously fruitful that they can't dismiss it, they will say that they are writing anti-novels, creating anti-theater or anti-art: better to deny art altogether than to admit that theirs isn't absolutely superior.

We find it annoying to read a newspaper that doesn't reflect our opinions; we feel full of hostility toward people we've never seen but whose way of life is different from ours. During periods of social crisis, we even support the idea that our adversaries should not be allowed to demonstrate, speak, write, or "disturb

---

*There are a number of new artistic schools in France — the New Theater (Ionesco, etc.), the New Cinema (Truffaut and the New Wave), and the New Novel (Robbe-Grillet, Butor, etc.).

the peace.'' Some people don't hesitate to resort to open violence, punitive raids, or bombings. I have derided the clergy for their excesses, but we should not forget that they are the most common target of such abuse and that they have, historically, endured more of it than any other social group. That's because they are the representatives of the reciprocal spiritual worlds. But order has to be preserved at any price, and anything that threatens to compromise it has to be destroyed.

Dependence on a rule, like dependence on a living being or dependence on an object, has similar consequences. The object provided varies, but the behavior of both individuals and groups is more or less the same. ''I miss you,'' ''I'm in need,'' ''They need everything,'' ''You're not doing your duty'' — it is no accident that each of these statements refers to something missing.

Dependence on reason strongly resembles dependence on irrationality. There is a rationalist fanaticism and an irrationalist fanaticism. Some rationalists claim that reason is infallible, and they will do anything within reason to defend it. Of course, things aren't that simple. The struggle for the triumph of reason is often the symbol of a more complex battle. Jacobinism and the philosophy of the Enlightenment, like the Inquisition and the Crusades, also had economic and political significance. But, in fact, things are never simple. Rationalists have a need to believe in a transparent world that can be mastered with an all-purpose tool; if they don't believe that, they will panic and go on the offensive. The Islamic war against the infidel, in which the Islamic peoples forced those they conquered to convert, giving them a choice of ''conversion or death,'' wasn't just a reflection of their desire to gain power through expansion but also a reaction to the anguish they felt when they saw other people adoring other gods and observing other rites. If the gods worshipped by other people are good, if other people are righteous and their opinions valid, then what does that make our god and what is the value of our customs? The citizens of one country will speak derisively about the customs of another, but they find it intolerable when someone else does the same thing to them. They make light of the disasters that strike their neighbors, but they doctor their own history, omitting any mention of unpleasant or dishonorable events and transforming defeats into victories, retreats into brilliant tactical maneuvers, distinguished persons into superhumans, and heroes into saints. Legend takes up where history leaves off and presents the past in the best possible light for eternity. And if dissertations and the resources of the imagination aren't enough, people will protect and consolidate collective dependency relationships with sword in hand. This tendency is responsible for a great deal of the aggressive behavior that human beings customarily exhibit. Every race of people has always, throughout its history, vigorously defended its symbols against those of others and its faith against other faiths, destroying, if necessary, the visible traces of foreign cultures and religious worship. After a war, those who have been victorious construct altars in the very same locations where the altars of the vanquished population formerly stood, as if it were imperative that no trace of the originals should be allowed to remain. In Morocco it used to be the custom for a new sovereign to immediately destroy his predecessor's palace. Isn't that just what modern political regimes do when they go to great lengths to mislead the public about previous regimes so that history will, from that point on, be written the way they want it to appear?

When the people of one nation destroy the temples, palaces, and gods of another or confuse their genealogies and rob them of their collective memory, which happens in colonization and in most domination, they don't, of course, ask themselves how the other people feel. In high school we were taught to admire

Dependence

Polyeuctus,* for his destruction of the pagan temples and the great achievements of the colonial army. At the entrance to the Arab quarter of Tunis, a statue of Cardinal Lavigerie stood as a reminder of the triumph of Christianity over Islam. We were never given any idea of the anguish and silent fury that those who worshipped in the ancient temples must have felt when they witnessed the destruction of their sanctuaries and protective gods; nor was it ever suggested that the colonial subjects of our own time, who were forced every day to pass by the representative of a foreign god or a statue of the conqueror, felt the same emotions. It is not surprising, then, that the first thing the citizens of a newly liberated nation do is to destroy the symbols of their subjection and reestablish their own objects provided.

Termination Rituals: Exorcism

Despite all our elaborate precautions, it is impossible to avoid all the real or imaginary terminations that lie in our paths. Some terminations are inevitable, and some are even necessary, victories and not catastrophes. Terminations are sometimes essential for the success of an enterprise, for personal growth, or for self-realization. A person has to know how to make a break and has to have the courage to do so.

If an object provided is no longer beneficial, the best thing is to get away from it. Put it out of your life, or escape from it — fight against your need for it. This is known as exorcism, the contrary of and antidote for possession. Possession is a kind of dependence; and exorcism is a method of liberation. Jealousy leads to the destruction of the object provided and to self-

---

*St. Polyeuctus of Melitene (Armenia), a fanatical Christian beheaded by the Romans in 259 A.D. He was the hero of an important play by the seventeenth-century French dramatist Pierre Corneille.

destruction. Exorcism, which is more efficacious, aims at the transformation of the dependent. But that transformation involves a certain amount of pain and danger. Fortunately for the individual, she doesn't always have to fight this difficult battle by herself. Most societies have developed termination tactics to help the societies themselves break out of dependency relationships that have become intolerable or to help individuals who are imprisoned in such relationships, who are so possessed by them that they become paralyzed or panic-stricken and unfit to fulfill their social obligations.

When we hear the word *exorcism*, we usually think of magic. Exorcists are associated with sorcerers and healers, and ethnologists have shown the importance of possession and exorcism for numerous primitive tribes. But exorcism is a mechanism that is expressed in a great variety of ways and is common to a multiplicity of social contexts. There is, indeed, a clerical and religious exorcism that is still practiced today. The Christian exorcist is a priest who acts with the consent of his superiors and according to a codified ritual. He has a mission: to combat the devil and his different incarnations. The Jewish tradition recognizes the existence of a *dibbuq*, or spirit of a dead person that occupies the soul of a loved one. Exorcism takes the form of more or less amiable negotiations with the devil, or *dibbuq*, who eventually goes away and gives the possessed person his or her freedom again.

Modern psychotherapists deal with essentially the same phenomena, under different names and, despite appearances, with similar methods. What is hypnosis — which was the first method employed by Freud — but a way of suggesting to the patient behavior that is more in accordance with his own needs and the exigencies of his environment? Hypnosis is unsound, almost self-contradictory, in that it proposes to increase the subject's capacity for independent action without requiring him to exercise his will, which is subordinated to the will of the hypnotist. It is true that the will of a patient who is possessed is not entirely free. Such a person is temporarily incapable of resisting the spirit, devil, or evil thoughts that have taken up residence inside him. The most innovative aspect of psychoanalysis is the attempt to get the subject involved by reeducating his will, so that he can once again be free to make decisions about himself and about other people. To accomplish that, the therapist simultaneously pursues two different objectives: the reinforcement of the subject's ego and the demythologizing of the origin of the conflict, that is, a more accurate view of the object provided, its relative devaluation, and, sometimes, its disappearance.

*

If we examine religious rituals, we see that they are designed to achieve the same two objectives as noted above. What are prayer and good works but ways of constantly reinforcing the soul to increase its freedom with respect to the world? While everyone is familiar with the procedures by which objects are consecrated, it is less well known that there are also procedures by which things can be deconsecrated. Before a stole or candelabrum can be sold to a secondhand store or junk dealer, a priest has to transform them from sacred objects into things that are merely profane. The transformation signifies that he divests them of their specific power, which in this case is the power to satisfy the spiritual needs of a dependent. Wine that has been consecrated becomes the blood of Christ; when it is deconsecrated, it becomes ordinary wine again. Once a candlestick that has been used on the altar is deconsecrated by a priest, it becomes just an everyday device for providing light. Among Jews any crumbs of bread that have not been swept up by the woman of the house before Passover begins have to be neutralized, with a special prayer, by the father of the family; after Passover, bread is just bread again and the faithful resume the practice of gathering up the slightest bits of crust and putting them into cracks in the wall or on windowsills.

*

There is a certain affinity between people who are possessed, people who are hypnotized, people who are neurotic, and people who are dependent. In making such a grouping I don't mean to suggest that those who are dependent are not worthy of our respect, but merely that we are all more or less impeded by that which takes place inside of us, of which we're largely unaware. A person who is possessed believes herself to be subject to a will other than her own, which seems to be inside of her. A person under hypnosis is commanded by the will of the hypnotist, which he has provisionally internalized. A neurotic is immersed in her conflicts, which she doesn't clearly perceive and which prevent her from living. A person who is dependent may be conscious of his dependence, but his will, if it isn't already part of the problem, is powerless to do anything about it.

Anyone who wants to help any of these people will use techniques developed through trial and error by laypeople and taken up and adapted by priests and doctors, all designed to accomplish the same thing. The person giving the help can try to break the ties that bind the patient by working either on the patient or on the object. This requires both science and tact. While it is necessary to understand the problem, it is also important that the patient's anguish at the separation be graduated, that the termination be accomplished in stages. When the cord is cut, the patient's flesh should not, through ineptitude, stupidity, or brutality, be torn as well. Once the relationship between the dependent and her dependence has been slowly transformed, the patient will accede to a new state in which she will see things differently and act differently. A prudent approach to the problem will effect the transition without exposing the patient to any danger.

Rites of Passage

Change is generally painful; the passage from dependence to relative freedom, or even from one kind of dependence to another, from one object provided to another, is a source of anxiety. So we have to anticipate it, prepare its stages, and mark out its course. Rites of passage serve as milestones along the route followed by the individual in his struggle through life. The life of every individual is punctuated, charted, and bounded by these treasured landmarks. Ceremonies, celebrations, prayers, formal acts of thanksgiving, the sharing of secrets, and initiations help the novice to confront his change in status without too much apprehension. Gifts, new clothes, insignia, and new prerogatives illustrate and give concrete evidence that the individual is breaking with his past and turning toward a future that is as full of promises as it is of risks. Among Muslims, the ritual of circumcision symbolizes at once, in an extraordinary condensation and right on the flesh of the preadolescent boy, the pain that is an inevitable aspect of every termination, the child's emergence from the indulgent world of women and his glorious but frightening entrance into the society of men. To alleviate the solitude that envelops the candidate in the face of this trial, his elders organize this memorable day so that he feels more confident. If all goes well, the praise he gets from the men and the admiration he gets from the women, all the happy and solemn aspects of the ceremony, will convince him that he is worthy of the world of difficulties, and also of victories, to which he has been admitted. That is just what it takes to transform a little boy into a future citizen. The Christian sacrament of First

The Dependent and Dependence

Communion and the Jewish bar mitzvah are designed to achieve the same results: working-class people commemorate such occasions by giving the child his or her first watch or pen. All the ceremonies that surround the celebration of a marriage — the traffic between the houses of bride and groom, the words and written communications they exchange, the gifts their families give each other, and the promises they make — are symbols of that same dialectic of passage. A girl leaves her adolescence behind her and blossoms into a woman, a wife, and, before long, a mother; a boy becomes the head of a family, a husband, and, before long, a father. Two groups of people each lose one of their members in order to give birth to a third group; two young people who only yesterday didn't have a care in the world are going to be responsible, economically, socially, and culturally, for someone else. All this is cause for rejoicing; it is blessed and celebrated by all concerned, with the result that the bride and groom go through the period of rapid adjustment in a sort of blissful trance. It is all serious, and the heroes of the adventure are surrounded, advised, encouraged, and assisted materially and spiritually until they get established on their own.

Every time anyone is about to enter a new, decisive stage in life, certain measures can be taken to prepare him or her. In my native country, whenever anyone was going off on a trip, we would spill a glass of water behind him so that he would be able to get back and would, because of this testimony, be assured that we would all be fondly awaiting his return. This meant that he would leave full of confidence. While he was gone, we would avoid doing or saying anything that might increase the distance and enlarge the seas that separated him from us.

Even the rituals and ceremonies associated with bereavement have the same purpose, although in this case it is not, strictly speaking, a question of a passage but of a one-way trip, because

143

Dependence

nothing can bring the deceased back to life. It is important, nevertheless, that some attempt be made to alleviate a pain so intense, a panic so desperate, that some people might not be able to bear up under it. That is why, throughout the world, the various cultures have made special efforts to deal with bereavement. They have taken upon themselves the difficult task of convincing individuals and groups that death is not the end of existence. They make use of funeral arts, memorial services, the inventions of religion and mythology, and popular beliefs to give the deceased a fictional existence, "another life." In some civilizations the people, in spite of everything, find the ordeal unbearable and the thought of an end to existence too over- whelming, and they prefer to deny death. They suppress the word that names it, never refer to it, and eliminate every material or symbolic trace of it.

The rituals associated with bereavement can also help people deal with problems other than death. Detoxification and weaning are miniature bereavements, because they are both situations in which there's no turning back. Every time a dependent suffers a permanent loss, she needs more help, a specific ritual of assistance. If the individual were left to her own devices, she would be helpless; in the face of the certitude that her loss was irreparable, she would conclude that it was useless to fight. Because they have understood that feeling of solitude and the lure of the abyss, people have organized various kinds of col- lective assistance, ranging from the ritualization of alcohol and hallucinogenic herbs common in primitive societies to the dif- ferent forms of group therapy employed today.

But sometimes nothing works — neither the dependent's own efforts nor help from others. Romantic disappointments some- times lead to death, and to say that someone "had a stroke" can sometimes be a literal, rather than figurative, description

144

of an event. "Lovesickness is a disease that doctors don't know how to cure," say the words of a song; "Losing money won't kill you," but sometimes it does. In the end, the dependent has to deal with his bereavement alone and he is the one who has to pay the consequences. So it is up to him to decide for himself what he will be able to tolerate without too much harm. You have to know how to make a break, it's true — if you can. Sometimes the advantages you gain by being courageous are not very important compared with the disorder and destruction that result; in such cases, it just isn't worth it. When all is said and done, it is sometimes better to perpetuate a questionable dependency relationship than to tear your heart out and destroy your spirit. And often the generous thing to do is to understand and respect other people's dependency relationships and not to criticize them in the name of morality.

III
The Use and Abuse
of Dependence

Dependence and Freedom

On the whole, the real problem of dependence is not its existence or nonexistence or the manner in which the moralist views and judges it. Its specificity is undeniable; its importance, which varies with the individual, is indisputable for all human beings, and probably for animals. We should ask ourselves not whether we can avoid being dependent, but how to be dependent.

Not that dependency doesn't pose serious ethical and philosophical problems. We have the right to put forth complete autonomy, of the individual and of groups, as an admirable and necessary ideal. To be independent of any person, any object, any soil or community, any tradition or project, any activity or passion can appear to be perfect wisdom or great strength of character. Some have supported that idea, at least as something to aim for on the infinite horizon of human existence. But does that correspond to the reality, even potential, of life as we live it? A priest questioned by André Malraux on his experience of confession replied, "There's no such thing as an adult." One of our professors at the Sorbonne, an eminent philosopher of science, once asked himself in front of us, "Who is an adult?" If to be an adult is to acquire complete autonomy, then no one has ever been an adult, no invividual or group. To believe the contrary is to live an illusion more harmful than having an awareness of your limitations. Anyone who has closely observed other people knows that for everyone there is always, somewhere, dependence. The anarchist who proclaims and has tattooed on his chest, "Neither God nor Master" will also manifest his absolute faith in camaraderie, that is, his need for his friends.

In the final analysis, what does it mean to be free of dependence on any thing or any person? We might say that it means having no need of any thing or any person. When you come right down to it, does that still make any sense? I must admit

149

Dependence

that the idea of absolute freedom seems vain to me, as much from the ethical as from the psychological point of view. On the collective level, we soon discover that total independence is nothing but a phrase, at best a manifesto or piece of nostalgia. The sublime cry of all the great struggles — "Liberty or death!" — is too pretentious to escape disappointment, even after victory. Events never fail to slightly attenuate the savage exigency of the slogan. Perhaps it's just as well: excessive purity is rarely compatible with the elementary welfare of nations. If the early days of revolutions are often exciting, they are also quite difficult to live. On the individual level, is a person who asks for nothing and gives nothing admirable, or just enviable? Isn't there something a bit sad in what appears to be a challenge: "I don't need anyone!"? Doesn't this also mean: "I don't want to ask for help from anyone because I'm afraid it will be refused"? Or "Because I'm afraid I won't be able to pay the price"? Beyond the vanity of the proclamation, that professed independence most often conceals a multitude of unacknowledged dependencies.

Finally, would it be desirable, if one could, to be completely independent? The quest for a provider is not a sign of independence, but neither is the total rejection of dependence an obvious sign of freedom. It is a fear of depending, that is, a fear of others. Whoever instinctively refuses the help of another is in her heart afraid of coming into contact with the other. The gift may be poisoned bait that will set off the trap in which she'll be caught. But every offer is not a trap; it is usually a bargain. Accepting a relative dependence can be an indication of confidence in oneself and in one's peers. Doesn't a person who never relies on anyone else deprive himself of everyone and everything? Of all the benefits and of all the emotional rewards that arise from reciprocal needs?

The Role of Dependence

Above and beyond what is possible and desirable, the fact remains that *no one can ever be totally independent.* That is the truth and the reality of the human condition.

The need for others may be specific and innate, or it may derive from other fundamental needs, but it is clear that children, to develop, need other people. They need other individuals to begin with — namely, their mothers and fathers — then, very soon, the various other people; soon after that, the whole collective: objects, institutions, and values. And almost every human being will always have these needs.

The proof that this is true is the fact that, if these needs are not satisfied, there will be disorder, malaise, suffering, and sometimes disorganization or even death. Those who don't have the usual attachments are most often unhappy people, people whom others, to make matters worse, suspect and condemn. There is something shocking, and even pejorative, about celibacy. How can anyone be celibate? How can anyone not want to have children? What hidden impediment keeps such a person back, what imperfection or vice? In reality, however, celibacy is a sort of neutral state that should not be perceived as a problem. But people find it more comprehensible and normal that married couples should stay together and wage constant war against each other. That's because they understand how such couples feel about their situation. Divorce would be a terrible ordeal. All separations are painful, even if they ultimately bring relief. And most of all: "Living with you is hell, but living without you would be like living in a desert; anything is better than solitude." Isolation is considered a catastrophe, and those who have been left alone feel as if they've been struck by one. The correlation between solitude and suicide attempts is undeniable, although there are undoubtedly other factors that are equally important in suicides.

151

Dependence

*

If you take away a person's affections for others, his job and his form of recreation, what is left? Isn't prison so miserable because the inmates are deprived for a long period of time of the opportunity to participate in the usual dependency relationships? Some people, after a few years of imprisonment, remain permanently marked by this deprivation. One of the things that makes life more difficult for patients in a hospital, who have to cope with the disruption of their usual routine, inactivity, strange surroundings, and a schedule that requires them to get up, eat, and retire at the oddest hours, is the lack of daily contact with their families. Albert Schweitzer was ridiculed for letting the relatives of his patients camp on the grounds of his hospital. But that policy reflected a valuable insight. If life in hospitals could be made more like life outside, it would be beneficial not only to the patient but also to the hospital staff, who would be relieved of some of their overwhelming responsibility.

*

When the transformation seems irreversible, when an individual's dependency relationships have come to a permanent end, it is time to fear the worst. Even simple doubt can sometimes be fatal. Some creative people, fearing, right or wrong, that they can no longer paint or write, commit suicide. That happened to Montherlant, who had gone blind; it probably also happened to Ernest Hemingway, to the painter Nicholas de Staël, and to Strauss, the musician. Since they were no longer certain that they could continue to create, life seemed intolerable.

This is what makes old age so tragic. Although elderly people do, of course, have to cope with the deterioration of their senses and decreased mobility, they suffer most of all from the progressive loss of their ties to other people. Their spouses have died, their children have gone out on their own, they have lost touch with all the people they used to work with, and their friends are either dead or close to death. They're experiencing the final psychological agony that prefigures physical death. What is a personality, a human character, but those complex webs that individuals weave around themselves and that bring meaning, joys, and sorrows into their lives? Without them, life is all silence, immobility, and neglect, and before long individuals start to fall apart, like abandoned factories, and resign themselves to death. The problem for elderly people is not that they come to be controlled by others but that others are not there when they need them most. Just as they're about to get helpless, they find themselves alone. That is why elderly people so often return to the religion of their childhood, even if they never practiced it as adults. At this point in their lives, religion is their only hope; and, for all we know, it may be the only kind of help they can get by simply deciding that they want it: "Ask and you shall receive."

Dependence has a role to play in life. At the very least it keeps us from becoming isolated, from destroying ourselves, and from thinking too much about death. It prevents us from becoming excessively introspective and from dwelling too much on what might happen in the future. People can hardly play, nor can they always "keep busy," all alone; and when people gather together, they not only enjoy having company but also protect each other from anguish. Also, the best way to solve practical problems is to find out, by exchanging information, how other people have solved them. After all, we satisfy a great many of our vital needs in the course of our commerce with others — emotional as well as purely economic needs.

Reciprocity

On the whole, dependence is one of the basic elements of the

Dependence

bond that ties one member of a society to another. Dependence expresses the nature of that bond better than anything else, better by far than dominance, which can't endure without dependence. The best way to dominate someone is not to rely on your own strength but to make the person you want to dominate dependent. Because they have understood this principle, Americans and, to a lesser extent, Russians have been able to take up where French and English colonialists have left off. Instead of sending out expeditionary forces to subdue the former colonial subjects, they have offered to attend to some of their needs. The satisfaction of needs prepares the way for dependence; and *reciprocal need,* that is, the need for one another, creates the conditions that lead to regular commerce.

It is not ethics, the moral law, or any supernatural commandment that perpetuates communal existence. Philosophy, ethics, the moral law, and religion explain, order, legitimate, and prescribe the essential connection that keeps societies functioning. Dependence is the expression of the permanent reciprocity that, because of their needs, exists between most of the members of a group: dependence of the weak on the strong, but also of the strong on the weak; dependence on providers by those who have nothing, and the opposite. The global societies of the world, which is what people call France, England, and Germany, persist today because, over and above conflicts based on class and the various social antagonisms, the majority of people in France, England, and Germany feel that it's to their advantage to get along with one another and, when all is said and done, they act accordingly.

Solidarity, which keeps groups, from the smallest to the largest, together, is also a form of reciprocal dependence. A mother protects her child, but the child also protects the mother, emotionally and socially, in her relationship with her husband, with society, and with herself. She needs her child to get recognition in these relationships. We have all at one time or another witnessed, to our amazement, the spectacle of a young mother crossing a street jammed with traffic. Pushing her carriage along in front of her, while her baby sleeps inside, she cuts through the rush of people and vehicles like Moses crossing the sea with the Scriptures wrapped in his arms. She's sure that nothing will happen to her, and nothing does: pedestrians get out of her way and drivers slow down their cars.

The fact that men have always dominated women has obscured the fact that they are mutually dependent, but, in a fundamental sense, men need women as much as women need men. The history of the species has been that men solve the problem of dependence by dominating women and women solve it by subjecting themselves to men. When a man needs a woman he takes, buys, or seizes her, to make her his companion or his thing; but he immediately begins to respond to her needs, especially her need for him to satisfy her desire for children. When a woman needs a man she seduces him and persuades him to take her, to satisfy his need for her. But both partners have a need, and it is not inconceivable that both needs might be satisfied by an arrangement based not on force and deception but on consensual reciprocal dependence.

Relationships in which one person dominates another are created by force and are therefore unstable; they invite revolt. Dependence is a stability factor whose destabilization produces the contrary effect: suffering. People who have been involved in dependency relationships react violently to separation and neglect, with occasional tragic results. Doctors engaged in the general practice of medicine know that when they go on vacation, some of their chronically ill patients will die, not from lack of care, since the doctors get others to replace them, but because the patients let themselves die. In extreme cases the dependent may, out of panic or despair, destroy everything, including himself, just as Samson, blind and bound in chains, smashed the pillars of the temple and buried himself, along with his enemies, in the ruins.

Evaluating Dependence

The ultimate problem associated with dependence is deciding how the cost of it compares with the advantages it offers. The reasonable thing is not to reject and condemn all forms of dependence but to thoroughly weigh both sides of the equation. Those who heap disdain on people who are dependent, treating them as if they were willing slaves, emphasize only one aspect of the bargain: the price that has to be paid, which is often excessive. Such people minimize or refuse to consider the importance, or the necessity, of the advantage the dependent wants to gain.

The example that seems to prove that the moralists are right is addiction to drugs: minor drugs — tobacco, alcohol, tea, and coffee — or hard drugs, with their dramatic gradations — hashish, heroin, LSD, including prescription and over-the-counter drugs, the ingestion of which produces comparable effects with respect to toxicity, tolerance, and inurement. But the phenomenon of drug addiction can be described in simple terms. People take drugs for two reasons: to get relief from feelings of uneasiness and to get pleasure. When an addict, including the person who just smokes ordinary, commercial cigarettes, feels a need coming on, he knows that the usual uneasy feeling is not far away. He knows, from his many past experiences with the syndrome, that he has entered into a state of incipient deprivation, and he dreads what will inevitably follow. So he has to make a choice: either put up with the increasing pain or immediately resort to whatever will make it go away, which is what he usually does. Other people can criticize him for resigning himself to constant defeat or pity him because his actions have adverse effects on his own physical and psychological health and on the lives of the people around him. Other people can advise him to resist or demand that he do so. But, that's more easily said than done. He, unlike the others, knows from personal experience the horrors of deprivation. Resistance has its rewards, of course, but are they sufficient compensation for the sufferings and disorders that result from abstinence? What the dependent does is to evaluate the two solutions by weighing, on the one hand, the price he'll have to pay — he'll be endangering his own health, harming that of others, and humiliating himself to the detriment of his own self-image — and, on the other hand, the satisfaction of a need that refuses to go away. He generally chooses to pay the price because, compared to his desire for satisfaction, which keeps getting stronger and stronger, all the rest doesn't seem very important. But it isn't always true that the dependent has no choice. It sometimes happens that, having relinquished the idea of making the effort, he no longer thinks about anything but getting relief from the discomfort he is experiencing, which he is afraid will turn into panic. If the moralists who condemn dependence were to find themselves in this predicament, would they still deliver the same sermon? The answer would be obvious even if we didn't know that some of those who try to keep other people from being dependent do so because they are afraid they might fall into the same state of abandon themselves, which, as much as they fear it, they would like to do. How many people who profess to be contemptuous of sex are secretly fascinated by it?

This is only the negative aspect of dependence: the elimination of pain resulting from deprivation. The advantages can be strictly positive, or the price to be paid for them can be minimal. At-

Dependence

tending to a need is a pleasure in itself: we *satisfy* needs. When we prevent suffering, or make it go away, we get a certain satisfaction — relief. There are, moreover, pleasures that don't necessarily involve suffering. Dependence on music, even if the music is not especially refined, has hardly any disadvantages. Some people smoke and drink just "for pleasure," without becoming addicted to it. Those who smoke a single cigar after dinner or who drink only when someone else is buying a round, are not haunted by need and deprivation. Of course, even occasional indulgence in this sort of thing can have its price. If you go out and "tie one on," you may have a headache or trouble with your liver the next day. The person who smokes only one cigar a day may make his teeth turn yellow or may disturb those around him. In any case, there is pleasure; in any case, there is pain. Passion is a peak between the valley of death and that of unlimited bliss.

Unless we condemn all pleasure, it's always a question of evaluation. Making love is fatiguing as well as pleasurable; doing it too often keeps a person from devoting himself to other occupations or takes him away from activities that are more worthwhile. Religious leaders and political militants both, with good reason perhaps, disapprove of amorous excesses, which they consider to be a waste of strength and attention. But the man on the street is neither an ascetic nor a priest nor a political fanatic; should he be taken to task because he doesn't prefer the sublime to joys that are simpler, even if they appear to be dubious and vulgar? Besides, except in extreme cases he is fairly good at navigating between the Scylla and Charybdis of this particular strait.

Pathological Forms of Dependence

Dependence isn't an illness. If it were, everyone would be sick. But if dependence isn't an illness, it does nevertheless have its pathological forms. It can be excessive, or it can be defective;

that is, a person can be too dependent or not dependent enough. She can be so dependent that she can't live without her provider (whom she prevents, by this excessive dependence, from living himself), like a child who has just been born, or a paralytic, both of whom would die from hunger, thirst, and discomfort — not to mention external aggression — if they were left to themselves. Such extreme dependence is sometimes, no doubt, almost a matter for psychiatry. In most cases of this kind the subject is, fortunately, the victim of a phobia rather than a real incapacity. She thinks she could never get on a train and leave behind the person and place that represent security to her, but when she does, she finds out that the sky won't fall on her head. In the meantime, as long as she hasn't made such a move, she will feel caught in an imaginary net that has her imprisoned as surely as if it were steel. Fear can affect the most elementary bodily needs. A person can be afraid that she won't be able to breathe, that she won't be able to swallow food, and so on, which are obviously not real dysfunctions but manifestations of an underlying anxiety. Excessive or uncontrolled dependence can also have psychosomatic symptoms, which concern specialists in that kind of medicine as much as they concern psychologists.

A person may, on the contrary, be so independent that he no longer has any need for other people and, out of indifference or fear, avoids any contact with them. Such a person is on the way to becoming a victim of another kind of pathology: the deterioration or destruction of his emotional and social ties, with all the consequences such a development would have on his personality and on those around him. In an extreme case he might not be able to function as a member of society at all. If that happens, the excessively independent person will, strange to say, have come in a roundabout way to be in the same predicament as the person who is excessively dependent. Both the excessively

Dependence

dependent person and the totally independent person end up in the care of someone else. Total independence is usually an illusion. Anyone who thinks he is totally independent is simply refusing to acknowledge his dependence on others. The fact is that such a person is, in spite of himself, helped and supported by everyone. He is even more beholden to other people because he acts as if he weren't, like certain people who claim that they can do without everyone else and who are always asking others for help.

When dependence is pathological, it is always a case of some abnormality in the person's relations with other people. The pathological forms of dependence involve difficulties with autonomy or, conversely and complementarily, with separation. We know, especially from the work of psychologist René Spitz, * the great value of which is not diminished because it has since been completed and refined by others, that these difficulties have their genesis in childhood. Everything happens as if the separation of the child from its parents produced a veritable functional disorder which, if it lasts, and it is possible to determine how long it does, will result in a veritable toxicosis. This toxicosis, if events in the subject's life sustain it, will affect his entire adult existence. The need for other people, which begins in childhood, stays with us from birth to death.

Must we, therefore, make a choice? At first glance we get the impression that it would be better, if we could, to have too much autonomy rather than no autonomy at all. But that is far from certain. The lack of autonomy definitely means restriction, mutilation, and, in the end, more or less serious destruction of the personality. But excessive autonomy only seems to be

---

*René Spitz is a noted psychoanalyst who has studied the consequences of a child's separation from its parents.

equivalent to total freedom. It also ultimately means neglect, mutilation, and, eventually, disorganization.

Managing Dependence

All the evidence suggests that the healthy, wise course of action, the one to follow if you want to live in a state of relative normality, is to position yourself somewhere between the two extremes: to be dependent, but not excessively, so that you can extricate yourself if you have to and so that there can be reciprocity because life in society is based on reciprocity. The excessively dependent person hardly thinks of giving; and when one person in a dependency relationship does all the giving, there is always the danger that the other person will get lazy. A relationship in which there is no reciprocity is a threat to its own existence.

Is such moderation possible? Doesn't it contradict the very nature of dependence? A dependent is the prisoner of her dependence and, yet, she is supposed to control it. That sounds impossible, but it isn't. To take a comparison from the works of Plato, we are, whether we like it or not, led by our dependency relationships in the same way we would be led by a team of horses; precisely because of that, however, we can exercise some control over them. We can't very well stop the horses, but we can, by working on one horse at a time, moderate their pace and keep them from going off the road and dumping us in a ditch.

Between an impossible state of perfection, which is enjoyed only by gods or by a few rare heroes ("I am master both of myself and of the universe"), and a dependence so acute that it leads to paralysis, self-destruction, or aggression, there are as many possibilities as there are colors in the rainbow. Where there's life, there's love, and where there's love, there's insecurity. But you have to persuade yourself that a single failure, regardless of whether it is the dependent's or the provider's, does not nullify the love that two people have for each other. Or you must persuade yourself that both parties to a love relationship get something out of it: if one of the partners needs to be loved, the other needs to love. In a particular relationship, no one is exclusively a provider and no one is exclusively a dependent. And if, one day, it becomes necessary to terminate a relationship, you have to tell yourself that there is no such thing as an absolute loss or a definitive bereavement because, as experience consistently shows, no one is irreplaceable. You just have to find the strength to wait, for time is the true master of the passions.

We may not be able to suppress dependency relationships, but we can manage them. How? This is equivalent to asking how we can reduce the cost. There are not that many ways to do it: you either work on the dependence itself, or you work on the object provided. You curb your desire for a particular object, or you change to another object and another supplier. Reduce your consumption, or look for substitutes.

Austerity

Nothing could be more obvious: the more desires we have, the more dependent we'll be. What we have to do, then, is to work on our desires rather than on our needs because we can't suppress our fundamental needs and there aren't that many of them. In this respect the reaction of contemporary ecologists is sound, in accordance with the practical precepts of traditional ethics. Most religions and philosophies recommend that people control their desires — live in relative austerity — and they are prepared to show them how to do so. Buddhism advocates the annihilation of the passions, that is, anything inside of us that causes us to be irresistibly drawn to a creature or an object. Christianity, which experienced its most rapid growth at a time when the Roman world, in which desire was king, was falling apart, exaggerated the Jewish distrust of unsanctified desire. Love for people or things has to pass through God as intermediary — it has to be partially or completely sublimated. Even ethical systems based on empiricism or pragmatism, in which there is no *a priori* suspicion of desire and which recognize it as one of the goals of human behavior, still give it only a limited, selective, qualified endorsement. That includes those astounding systems in which paroxysms are used for individual liberation or for mystical purposes. This unanimity indicates not that these religions and philosophies lack originality but that they all realize that desire will come closer to serving its proper purpose in life if it is regulated and controlled. In short, most religions and philosophies, even those that include some forms of temporary madness, advocate self-mastery.

Conflicts Between Dependencies

Even if religions and philosophies did not advocate self-mastery, we would have to develop it anyway. As life takes its course, it creates and destroys dependency relationships, and we have to adjust to the changes that result. It may also force us to choose one dependency over another; while they often converge, there is competition among them. Conflicts between dependencies often put individuals or groups into extremely painful predicaments. Many people might easily support two amorous attachments, but social pressures or the dissatisfaction of one of their partners would eventually force such people to give one of the partners up. Driving an automobile is, for some people, a pleasure as well as a practical necessity. It gives them an outlet for their nervous energy, a way to work out their aggressions ("It relaxes me"), a feeling of power that enhances their self-image ("I like to drive fast"), and some compensation for the setbacks they have experienced during the day. At the same time, however, it is a source of additional nervous fatigue and of stress from the increased vigilance necessary in the hostile competition with other drivers. Some people try to deal with this specific anxiety by seeking help from tranquilizers, alcohol, tobacco, or medicines. But you can't resort to that kind of relief without impairing your ability to drive. In the case of alcohol, for example, the amount it takes to adversely affect a person's senses or motor reflexes, even if it varies from one individual to another, is rather small. It is a regular vicious circle, which those who are responsible for highway safety try to break by persuasion or by repression: "Drink or drive, but don't do both at the same time." And that goes for taking tranquilizers as well. The driver has to choose between the two objects provided: the car or the drug. But sometimes he needs both, one because of the other. Termination is necessary in this instance not because of negligence on the part of a provider, or because an object provided no longer exists, but because there's a conflict between two dependencies, a conflict that can be either external or inside the dependent himself.

*

People still talk today about the incident that, after generating a great deal of controversy as well as newspaper articles and books, became the subject of the popular film *Survive!* It involved the survivors of a plane crash who, stranded on the top of a snowy mountain without any means of communication, kept themselves alive by eating the flesh of the passengers who had died. Some members of the public strongly condemned the survivors, while others vigorously defended them. But neither the incident itself nor the consumption of human flesh that resulted was particularly unusual. An old seafarer's song tells the story of how those on board a sailing ship that had been immobilized by a lack of wind drew straws to see who would be eaten. The truth of the story is confirmed by the fact that, according to the song, the shortest straw was drawn by the youngest member of the crew. It was no accident that they preferred to sacrifice the weakest person in the group. People have eaten human flesh in many other similar circumstances. Those caught in sieges definitely ate children, but only with the understanding that no one would have to eat his or her own. It all comes down to a question of another scandal over dietary preferences, the origin of the scandal being a specific taboo: you don't eat human flesh. Anyone who violates this taboo is breaking off a dependence on certain values, which is why he or she feels guilty and full of anguish. Since those who read about the plane crash or saw the film became strongly identified with the survivors, they felt the same anguish, which turned into hostility toward the people involved. On the other hand, if the survivors hadn't eaten the cadavers of the other passengers, they would have perished. And everyone agrees that people have to try to save their lives.

Here again is a conflict between two dependencies: which one should have been given priority? The one that would, whatever the price might be, ensure the survival of a few individuals and, beyond them, that of anyone in distress? Or the one that preserved a certain image of humanity and was also based on the necessity for the survival of the species: under no circumstance should people devour one another; they should rely for their subsistence on other species, animal or vegetable? There is no solution for this conflict, and traces of its two components can be found in the collective memories of the various races. Human sacrifices, elevated to the status of ceremonies, periodically commemorate the crime of fratricide. Long after the destruction of Carthage, the goddess Tanit continued to demand the slaughter of children, whose carbonized bones have been found there. Many years later the Berbers, on the field of battle, would smear their faces with the blood of an enemy soldier, take a bite of his

Dependence

liver, chew it up and spit it out: that's all that remained of the barbaric practices that were once necessary for survival.

Substitution

It is obvious that austerity is not always enough. And since there are even times when we don't have a choice, we sometimes have to make up our minds that the only solution is abandonment, pure and simple — leave your provider or be left by him. Fortunately for us, our psychological resources are more numerous than we think; we can still deceive our dependencies. The second important method for dealing with the ordeal of termination is substitution, in which the emphasis is on the object provided: you persuade yourself that another object will do just as well. Since you can't do anything about your need for the object, you work on the belief that links you to it. The compulsory aspect of dependence is tempered by the interchangeability of objects provided.

One dependence displaces the other. The dependent, immersed in her dependence, does not immediately see this way out. From blindness or stubborn pride, she will initially refuse to take it. To do so would be to minimize the importance of her particular experience. Every fanatic is hypnotized by the object of her passion and thinks it is unique, irreplaceable; she puts it on a pedestal and has contempt for everything else. Fanatics are myopic. But those around them are not. Everyone knows, from personal experience or from what he has been told, that a person can fall in love several times during his lifetime, go into a different line of work or field of art, and even change his religion. The fanatic doesn't want to know that — for the time being; because before too long she will begin to see things as others see them. Before too long she will find a new object worthy of a new passion; she will allow herself to experience the same joys and the same painful fits of anger. Unless satiety — but is a passion that has been satisfied still a passion?

Of course, you can't make just any kind of substitution. Sometimes things that seem to be obvious equivalents don't work. The personal element is particularly important. For some people, one child can replace another; for others, each one is a unique source of joys and cares, and nothing, not even a very large family, can make them forget a single loss. There are definitely people who fall in love only once and women who become inconsolable widows: "I've had three boys and two girls, but believe me, nothing can replace my husband." Getting married again does not always make the memory of the first husband or wife go away. Even the most noble object cannot always eclipse an exceedingly humble one, as it does in sublimation, which is, in effect, an attempt to make a substitution. I have often discussed the problem of solitude with priests. It is my impression that neither prayer, which represents the hope of communication with a divinity, nor communal living, nor contact with the faithful can completely compensate for the lack of a privileged relationship with a woman. I don't mean just for the satisfaction of erotic needs; even when such needs are not a problem, there is still something missing. One priest told me quite frankly how painful it was for him to come home at night: "Even if I've seen a lot of people during the day, even if I've worked really hard. . .it doesn't make any difference." Just a minute before, he had tried to describe to me the intensity of the divine presence in his life and how it gave meaning to it; so much so, he maintained, that he couldn't live without it. I took the liberty at that point of asking him why God wasn't sufficient for him. His reply was humble: "I don't know; it makes me dissatisfied with myself, but that's the way it is." He convinced me, without actually saying it, that solitude is one of the main things a priest takes into consideration when he decides to leave the Church.

In spite of everything, there are, for each individual, substitutions that he doesn't realize he could make and that he can discover only by experience, trial and error, or chance. Smokers who can't get their favorite brand of cigarettes, for example, are sometimes pleasantly surprised to find another kind that they like just as much as, or more than, their regular brand. There are thousands of men or women in the world we could fall in love with; one attachment can, in effect, displace another. A single substitute may perchance have more than one kind of value: a piece of jewelry is an expression of love and is also worth money. The lucky person in this respect is the one who quickly finds a substitute that is more appropriate for him than any other, that doesn't cost him too much in terms of money or health, and that isn't too harmful to those around him.

Searching for the most appropriate substitute is, in any case, the best way of treating the disorders associated with dependence. You can't do much to stop people from smoking or drinking unless you find out why the smoker smokes and the drinker drinks, that is, why they are dependent in the way that they are. That is why most campaigns against smoking or drinking are relatively unsuccessful: they prohibit and dissuade, but they don't explain; they don't give the dependent what she needs; they don't really help her to replace, or even to control and master, her object provided.

Ritualization

Ritualization can be another convenient way of mastering dependence. By allowing it only at certain times, you prevent it from taking over the whole life of the dependent. A person would drink while eating but not between meals; he would smoke during the two or three long pauses that occur during the day and abstain the rest of the time. And if ritualization were given group approval, codified by religious or secular laws, the individual would feel both supported and restrained. That may be the best approach: collective ritualization. Many societies have adopted that solution. A carnival is an intense but temporary relaxation of the moral code; rituals that involve inebriation allow people to periodically experience the pleasure and disequilibrium that come from drinking alcohol. Other groups seem to prefer absolute prohibition. Islam completely forbids the ingestion of alcohol; one glass is enough to send a person to hell. It is the law of all or nothing, which is also endorsed by Alcoholics Anonymous. Such a law may be necessary in certain individual cases; chemistry will give us more precise information some day. But it is clear that both Islam and Alcoholics Anonymous tolerate other forms of dependence, forms that have been subjected to ritualization. On the whole, ritualization is freedom with surveillance, so it amounts to relative restraint. It allows the dependent to get relief through a relative transgression; at the same time, it assigns him limits without which the disorder would be in danger of becoming even more intolerable.

That's why an alcoholic or drug addict can find salvation through membership in a group when medicine so often fails: dependence on the group takes the place of dependence on the object — alcohol or drugs. In a way, it is only right. Alcohol served as compensation for a loss, a romantic disappointment, a deceased spouse or child, a failure at work, or a vanished hope. A relationship with another person had been replaced by a relationship with an object. Membership in a group helps put things back the way they were before: to restore the human relationship that had been destroyed.

Dependence

The Ideal Substitute

We should not get carried away: there's no miracle cure. It would be useless to imagine that we might someday be able to eliminate all undesirable consequences, all harm or emotional damage. That would be almost contradictory. It implies the possibility of a pure dependency relationship, which brings us back to the dependent person's golden dream: the absolute gift, lavished on the dependent by a totally disinterested provider — a romantic hero, mother-lover, or father-lover — and without any strings attached, without any inconvenience of any kind. There is no law against dreaming.

If we could develop for each situation a remedy that did not have any of the usual consequences, what a resource that would be! What a boon! To go with the all-purpose food pill, why not a pill that would alleviate, without enslaving anyone or subjecting him or her to unpleasant consequences, a person's hunger for love? Why not, while we're at it, a kind of "cure-all," which is just what quack doctors periodically try to sell to any half-skeptical, half-gullible member of the public who stops to listen? The novelist Aldous Huxley, in *Brave New World,* expressed the desire for such a thing. A world like the one imagined by Huxley would be the best of all possible worlds because people would finally have a universal remedy, which would take away all their cares. Would such a discovery really be desirable? What would become of a human race dependent on an all-purpose substance that could make life absolutely serene? The heart of the issue is the whole problem of anxiety — should there be just a little, a great deal, or none at all? Too much anxiety makes life unlivable, but is it certain that the total absence of anxiety is beneficial for the individual and for the species? Is it beneficial for creative people, for example? Or just for maintaining the impetus that has made humans the dominant creatures on earth and perhaps in the inhabited universe? Better to have the perpetual, fragmentary and diversified, constantly improved, and always insufficient process of refinement with which scientists have occupied themselves, especially during the last few decades.

It is also clear that every drug operates by producing a physiological shock — in order to counteract another one, it's true. But there is always the chance that its very efficacy will become a danger, unless it, in its turn, is kept under control. It can become a danger by virtue of its immediate as well as its long-range effects. Even if the drug is initially benign, the changes it introduces into the system, which start out to be salutary, can become pernicious. Even a caress, if it's repeated many times, will cause an irritation, then a lesion, of the skin. The solution would be to develop medicinal drugs that would be as benign as possible and, at the same time, to learn to do without them as soon as possible.

Is that all? If a great many forms of dependence were to be eliminated in favor of treatment with drugs, would that solve the problem? Not entirely. Because there is still positive pleasure, the pleasure that does not come just from the cessation of pain but is a kind of bonus. No pill for relieving hunger can replace the pleasure we get from eating; nor can sublimation, through devotion to a great cause, of the emotions that would ordinarily be associated with love for another person replace the exquisite feeling peculiar to that experience. Satisfaction is not the only kind of pleasure. There is also enjoyment — and why should we deprive ourselves of that? What ascetism obliges us to forgo such blissful states, whose variations dance above the water line, in joyous excitations, in sudden flashes toward enchanting exasperations? There will always be people who will be tempted by the delicious languors, the titillations and intoxications of pleasure, even if they can't afford it!

171

Dependence

The ideal substitute ought to be the equivalent of the object provided — but better, because it ought to have all the good qualities of the object, preferably multiplied, without having its defects. That sometimes happens. A second marriage sometimes opens the gates of heaven. Usually it's all in the mind: the person in question has simply chosen to overlook, for a time, certain defects, which he or she will eventually have to acknowledge. Many people who get divorced and then remarry even choose new partners who have a curious resemblance to their first ones. And sometimes, having learned the hard way that there is no such thing as a person without faults, they get divorced again, or end up resigning themselves to their fate. The point is that the ideal substitute is just that — an ideal — and *there's no such thing as a perfect substitute.*

In practice, each substitute solves a problem but leaves others in suspense, and even creates some. A substitute has to be the same and different; if it's different, however, it won't do exactly what the lost object did. That is clear in the case of sublimation, the replacement of a material object by a spiritual one. Divine love can be consolation for the risks associated with human love, or for its absence, but it can't completely replace it. It can't provide simple tenderness or satisfy the needs of the flesh. The problem is the same for any replacement. Artists who have devoted their life to their art sometimes wonder if they haven't sacrificed it. People have asked themselves what, in case of accidental or deliberate negligence, would be the ideal substitute for mother's milk. We know that mother's milk is extraordinarily well adapted to the physiology of the newborn child: its composition changes according to the evolution of the infant's needs. Even if someone managed to develop a substitute that was as rich, as versatile, and as suitable for its purpose, and that, dose for dose, had the same dynamic effect, the child would still miss the contact between his lips and the breast as well as the warm and enveloping presence of his mother.

In spite of everything that has just been said, *we should try to find ideal substitutes*. That is still the best way. The closer you get, the more likely it becomes that the operation will succeed. This has proved to be true with respect to the reeducation of people addicted to drugs and also applies to any kind of education involving sublimation, although we all know that felicity is not of this world. What is at work is perhaps one of the inexhaustible sources of human discontent: our tendency to yearn for a better life.

Practical Applications of Dependence

No method, no perspective can explain all of reality. I have not, therefore, in this portrait of the dependent, tried to reduce all human behavior and human works to products of dependency relationships, any more than I tried to explain the whole life of the dominated person in terms of his or her relationship with a dominator, although their lives are constantly intertwined. Politics is a collection of techniques for conducting society's affairs; art is a form of expression, communication, and research as well as a way of obtaining pleasure; religion is an instituion that regulates the relationships between the members of a society. But the fact remains that dependence plays a role in the lives of politicians, artists, and religious people and that a knowledge of the machinery of dependence helps make their works and behavior more comprehensible. There are political, artistic, and religious ways of responding to dependence. In this sense, dependence is definitely one of the most powerful and most efficacious of all the motives that generate human activity and one of the most fruitful concepts we have available to us as a key to its interpretation. It is no exaggeration to say that the

Dependence

consideration of dependence can help us formulate our ideas about politics, art, or religion, to develop a theory of education or, more generally, practical wisdom.

Once we turn our attention to the phenomenon of dependence, we can't help but recognize its importance. It is one of the ways in which human beings, in their relations with others and with the world around them, function to ensure their survival. The need that people have for things external to them is definitely a source of weakness, of various wants, and of permanent insecurity. Human beings are not sufficient unto themselves; they know that and are constantly experiencing the effects of it. The wisest course would undoubtedly be to find within yourself as much as you can of the strength it will take to make you self-sufficient. There will still be enough irrepressible needs, for which help from outside will be necessary. We have to gracefully accept such needs, which vary from person to person, and give them their due. We should frankly acknowledge our dependency relationships and cling to those in which there is no possibility of substitution.

Cling to them if we can be sure of them. But we never are completely and permanently sure of them. It is probably because of that fragility, which is unsettling inasmuch as it leaves people vulnerable to unpredictable transformations of the conditions under which they live, that human beings are so restless. And it is because they're restless that they've done such an amazing amount of wandering, both geographical and spiritual. Humans are always on the move, constantly fabricating ideas, theories, and fictions as well as tools. Permanent dissatisfaction drives them to pursue lasting satisfaction, which is impossible. Dependence is a bottomless pit. We can console ourselves for the existence of this fundamental weakness by telling ourselves that nothing escapes from it: what other living thing, animal or vegetable, is completely self-sufficient? We can take a bit of pride in it: our dissatisfaction is also the source of all the rich complexities that are part of human life, one of the things that has driven the human race to make progress, to become frightfully powerful, and to triumph over all the other species.

Regardless of whether dependence is, on balance, a negative or positive aspect of our existence, we have to take it into account. Education should be preparation for life as well as the communication of information — and not only during childhood, but throughout adolescence and even from adulthood to old age, to the point that it helps the individual face death. Children have to be taught to endure a certain amount of solitude, to master the difficult art of living autonomously, because they have to be able, at times, to get along without other people. They have to know how to reach out to others when that is necessary, how to offer others their love. This permanent tension is even more pronounced in adolescence, a period characterized by expectation and defiance — expectation, which implies openness, trust and, ultimately, making demands; defiance, which meets with resistance, comes back stronger, and eventually becomes rebellion. These two quite divergent adolescent tendencies have to be treated with consideration, respected, reconciled. Adults, at certain times, will have to keep their distance to avoid falling into the traps that spring up when they are trying to cope with the anguish of separation; at other times they will have to reach out to other people who are experiencing that anguish, to try to fill up the excruciating void in their lives. That's the essence of the contract that binds people to one another. There is a great deal of talk these days about gerontology, which is a trend that should be encouraged. The search for a solution to the problems of the elderly ought to proceed along the same lines as the education of children: people have to prepare themselves for old age, to learn, little by little, to cope with the solitude that inevitably creeps into their lives and, at the same time, not only try to maintain the ties they already have but even form new ones. If we want to reduce the incidence of death among newly retired people, we have to allow them to leave their jobs by stages rather than all at once, to adjust the mix of leisure and activity to the needs of the individual.

Dependence is not an illness and we wouldn't have anything to gain from making it into more of a medical problem than it is, or, for that matter, from suggesting that those who are dependent should feel terribly guilty. But because there do exist pathological forms of dependence, we have to develop a treatment for them. No program designed to foster mental health can be sound, no political system effective, that ignores the duality that makes individuals and groups feel and act in contradictory ways. Why do so many men and increasing numbers of women, even though they are married, continue to chase after members of the opposite sex, like domesticated Don Juans with a permanent thirst for romance? Some day we are definitely going to have to reconsider our attitude toward such behavior, that is, look at it more courageously.

The question of cultural identity is, as everyone knows, a popular subject of discussion right now. This exchange of opinion would certainly be more fruitful if it took dependence into account. There is nothing wrong with self-affirmation, but is it really necessary to cling so tenaciously to the customs and traditions of our own particular group? Membership in a group is a source of satisfaction — "We feel comfortable with people like us" — but we have to be careful not to exclude people who "don't come from here." Once we do, xenophobia, hate and fear, is not far behind. We should reject autarky and rehabilitate commerce — not just the exchange of ideas, as if it could be carried on all by itself, without an exchange of objects! More generally, social philosophy should never forget that human beings are dependent; not only does every individual have an imperious need for others, but others need him or her as well. That fact is a permanent reminder of the necessity for cooperation among the people of the world, as permanent at least as the distrust and vigilance that fester within a human race that has yet to emerge from barbarism.

Finally, a close study of the mechanisms of dependence is undoubtedly the best introduction to practical wisdom, individual or collective. A system of practical wisdom based on dependence would be more fruitful than one based on fear, anguish, and aggression. This isn't meant to deny the importance of the other dimensions of the human character, which are probably just as elemental as dependence. Some people have maintained, for example, that there is such a thing as a real instinct to dominate; others have defended the thesis that aggressiveness is congenital and therefore insurmountable. We will discuss these important questions some other time. Even if such theories were correct, aggressiveness and domination come into play in connection with the satisfaction of needs. People may very well wage war just for the fun of it, or to assert themselves individually and collectively, but usually it is to get material goods, to ensure the security of those they already have, and to dispose of threats. In other words, dominance is usually a response to dependence rather than a cause of it. A political economy based on dependency relationships, that is, on the satisfaction of needs, would in itself help to relieve us of some of our natural aggressiveness.

But that wouldn't solve everything; it wouldn't completely pacify the human race — perhaps nothing ever will. Fear and anguish have been part of our history for too long. Life, in any

Dependence

case, is an enterprise full of risks because death can end it at any time and because there is always the possibility that something essential for survival will be lacking. The fear of want is the most frightening specter that haunts our individual and collective memories. But we can try to exorcise it: that would save us a great deal in terms of battle, tears, and blood. As far as progress is concerned, there will always be enough of the old anxiety to keep the human race in a constant state of agitation.

Whenever anyone is elaborating a theory of any kind, there is a point at which it becomes tempting to develop it into a philosophy. We are at that point right now; and that's as far as we'll go. But we already have the broad outlines of a philosophy of human nature that would take into account not only the ways in which people dominate one another but also the many ways in which they depend on one another. A human being is definitely, as philosophers would say, a being-with, a being-in-relation.

APPENDIX
A Definition of Dependence

This appendix contains just a few remarks on the four key words of this book, with particular reference to *dependence* and to the definition I propose to give it. Because it is impossible to think clearly if we fail to preserve the purity of our language, I felt that I ought to define the terms so that each would have a single unequivocal connotation.

Take the diptych formed by domination and subjection. Everyone knows that we routinely refer in our speech to both "the domination of the powerful" and "the domination of the weak." The elasticity of this particular item in our vocabulary is the source of much confusion: we have to make a clear distinction between domination as an *activity* and domination as something *endured*. I suggest that the word *domination* be used exclusively to refer to what emanates from those who dominate with respect to those who are dominated and never to refer to what those who are dominated endure. *Domination is the totality of the constraints imposed by those who dominate on those who are dominated.*

The same, or almost the same, confusion reigns with respect to *subjection*. I suggest that this term be applied exclusively to what is experienced by those who are dominated. Subjection is, of course, the consequence of domination, but it is also more than that. There are specific, often unforeseeable, ways in which those who are dominated can respond to those who are dominating them. *Subjection is the totality of the ways, both active and passive, in which those who are dominated can respond to the aggressive behavior of those who are dominating them.*

If we now compare the two diptychs formed by dominance and subjection on the one hand and by dependence and providing on the other, it becomes clear that the equation involving dependents and their providers is not superimposable on the equation involving those who dominate and those who are dominated, even if this or that form of behavior closely ap-

Dependence

proximates another. *Providing is responding to the expectations of a dependent.*

*

What is a dependent being and why this word *dependence?*

If you are faced with the problem of giving a name to a collection of phenomena heretofore only dimly perceived, you can either create a new word or adopt an existing word and take the risk of proposing a new connotation for it. Each solution has its advantages and disadvantages.

I had chosen the first alternative when I created *Judaity* to designate "the fact and manner of being a Jew" and *negrity* for "the fact and manner of being black."* *Judaity* was widely accepted by the public, but there was some hesitation about *negrity,* despite the fact that it was welcomed by Léopold Sédar Senghor, one of the inventors of *negritude,* which, moreover, it was never my intention to replace but only to refine and complete. The reception was not so enthusiastic for *altero-phobia,* which I had hoped would replace *racism. Racism,* it seems to me, implies that biology is the only pretext people use when they accuse and reject a particular group, which isn't true. The problem with trying to introduce new words is that their novelty, which shocks the eye and ear, requires too much immediate effort on the part of the public.

In choosing *dependence,* a term that is already familiar, I am opting for the second solution, which seems easier on the reader. The price, this time, is the opposite disadvantage: since words always carry with them traces of the different contexts in which they've been used, the risk of ambiguity is greater. It would have

---

*To be more precise, each term was to be part of a trilogy: Judaity — Judaicity — Judaism; negrity — negricity — negrism; and, in the same order of ideas: Arabity — Arabicity — Arabism. I created these words in *Portrait of a Jew.* I used them also in *Dominated Man* in Chapter 3, "Negritude and Jewishness."

been impossible, for example, to use, as I once thought I might, *alienation*. I would have had to spend considerable time divesting the word of its theological, economic, and psychiatric connotations. In the course of being used in different ways, it has become too rich and too vague; it blurs the distinction between subjection, which it suggests, and what I mean by dependence, which would be at the very most a subtle form of subjection without a master — unless you equate providing with domination, which isn't always possible by any means. If you consider the way the word *alienation* is used by Marxists, it is unclear whether it's meant to refer to human beings in the universal sense — essentially, human groups — or to concrete individuals. Marxism properly applies only to groups; it is a theory about the domination of one class by another, and its ethic is based on the absolute necessity for destroying that domination. This is, moreover, quite enough. On the contrary, I am convinced that it would have something to gain from including dependence.

I was also tempted to borrow a term from psychology: *attraction, clinging,* or, better still, *attachment,* which was first used in Great Britain by John Bowlby and which has enjoyed a certain success in France thanks to the efforts of my colleague René Zazzo.* I had to give up that idea as well. I would have been saddling an otherwise useful concept with a supplementary connotation that would have made it even more imprecise. And I would also have been restricting the scope of dependence to the limits of attachment. In opposition to *alienation,* which is too broad and

---

*John Bowlby, author of *Attachment, Loss, The Making and Breaking of Affectional Bonds,* and *Separation: Anxiety and Anger,* is an English psychologist who has worked on the idea of attachment. René Zazzo is a French psychologist who has taken up Bowlby's theories. They have both shown that there exists between mother and child a very strong bond which they call attachment.

Dependence

ambitiously philosophic, *attachment* is too much a part of the vocabulary of psychology. Because it describes a trait that is undeniably part of the individual psyche, it would be inadequate, or at best analogous, for collective phenomena. Can we, without being metaphorical, say that one group is attached to another? An even more serious difficulty is that attachment does not account for one of the important characteristics of dependence: ambiguity. Attachment has, or at least the word has, an air of perfect positivity; dependence, despite all its advantages, is confusion and anxiety, and it is almost always simultaneously sought after and condemned. The ambiguity increases as we get further from our primary needs. All you have to do to convince yourself of that is to listen to fanatics talk about the object of their passion.

This duplicity is often brought out by psychoanalysis, which remains one of the most fruitful methods of investigating and interpreting the psyche. And no one should be surprised if we sometimes employ methods similar to those employed by that discipline, which has entered the public domain. But if dependence definitely gains from recourse to the methods of psychoanalysis, a reading of psychoanalysis according to the schemas of dependence would not exactly be a waste of time either. What is a conflict but an involvement in contradictory dependencies? What is psychotherapy but reeducation designed to put the subject back on his or her own feet again? The technique of transference is the manipulation of a substitute. The term *dependence* does appear in Freudian texts, but there is no sustained description or explicit conceptualization of it. Another difference, the last one we consider, is that psychoanalysis, despite the belated efforts of its founder and then of some of his disciples, has never been very convincing in its interpretation of group behavior. It isn't particularly well equipped for that task, any more than Marxism is particularly well equipped for the interpretation of individual behavior.

When all is said and done, it is better for everyone to hoe his own row, for the common good, instead of following in the footsteps of others, which produces nothing new. That is why my aim has been not to suppress or replace that which exists but to add a few stones to the edifice. The whole idea is that there is something to be gained from considering dependence as a distinct phenomenon, and it deserves to be inventoried directly.

For all the reasons I have just mentioned, I came to the conclusion that *dependence* was the best term for what I wanted to describe; the reader will be the judge. The definition I propose for it:

Dependence is a relationship with a real or ideal being, object, group, or institution that involves more or less accepted compulsion and that is connected with the satisfaction of a need.

A definition is only a tool, an attempt to include, for the greatest operational efficacy, a maximum of meaning in a minimum of words. Which is to say that whoever creates a definition can always hope to perfect it and that I don't pretend, any more than I do for the term itself, to have found the best solution to the problem. Nor is this definition an *a priori* proposition; it is the result of a direct examination of the different concrete forms of dependence. Every abstract notion is, by virtue of being a generalization, as fragile as a bloated wineskin. Don't forget, we took as the starting point for this study a description of actual life situations that have several common mechanisms that can be grouped to form a single concept. And I can attest, in return, that the concept derived from this process has proven to be indispensable for the understanding of a central aspect of human reality.